THE UNSUSPECTED SLUMS

REVISITING THE SLUMS OF 1930S MELBOURNE

FRANK PREM

Wild Arancini Press
2026

Publication Details

Title:	*The Unsuspected Slums: Revisiting the Slums of 1930s Melbourne*
ISBN:	978-1-923166-48-6 (p-bk)
ISBN:	978-1-923166-49-3 (Interactive PDF)
ISBN:	978-1-923166-94-3 ((Fixed Layout EPUB)

Published by Wild Arancini Press
Copyright © 2026 Frank Prem
All rights reserved:

No part of this publication may be reproduced, stored in a retrieval system, or transmitted in any form or by any means, electronic, mechanical, photocopying, recording or otherwise, without prior written permission from the publisher and author.
A catalogue record for this book is available from the National Library of Australia.

Cover Concept: Wild Arancini Press

Did you not know that a circle turns upon itself?

Contents

Introduction 1

Preface 3
    Richmond 7
    West Melbourne 17
    Carlton 35
    Collingwood and Abbotsford 79
    Fitzroy 127
    North Melbourne 169
    South and Port Melbourne 211
    Other Places Other Slums 227

Conclusion 283

After Words 287
    Image Sources 289
    What Readers Say 319
    Author Information 323
    Other Published Works 325
    Index of Poems 327

The Unsuspected Slums

Introduction

During the 1980s, when I was one of only a few Community Psychiatric Nurses in Melbourne, I worked out of a small clinic in East Melbourne. We provided community-based psychiatric services across Fitzroy, Collingwood, Richmond and Carlton. Much of my job involved visiting long-term psychiatrically unwell clients where they lived: small flats, seedy boarding houses, and the ever-present high-rise towers built and managed by the Victorian Housing Commission until 1984.

Forty-eight high-rise towers – each sixteen or seventeen storeys tall – were sited across the inner city, accommodating refugees, migrant communities, poorer people and the chronically unwell. Most residents qualified for housing assistance and, in many cases, a disability support pension or other social benefit. There were hundreds of points of origin, hundreds of languages and dozens of communities in each tower.

Fast forward to the present, and the towers still stand, more decrepit now than they were then, and generally in a poor state. The Victorian Government has begun the slow process of emptying them, with demolition and rehousing intended. "Unfit for purpose" is the main justification put forward.

In one of my forays into Victoria's digital archives, I came across the work of a man named Frederick Oswald Barnett – an accountant by trade and a Methodist lay preacher by conviction. As a Bachelor of Commerce student in 1928, he visited an inner-Melbourne slum pocket and was shocked by what he saw, particularly the conditions in which young children lived. That experience became the basis of his 1931 thesis, later published as a small but influential booklet, *The Unexpected Slums*, in 1933[1].

With others, Barnett helped drive a reform movement aimed at improving life for slum children and, ultimately, eliminating the slums altogether. His advocacy led the Premier to establish the Housing Investigation and Slum Abolition Board, from which the Housing Commission of Victoria emerged in 1938. Barnett served as vice-chair until 1948.

What strikes me now – and what feels particularly pointed given current debates about Melbourne's high-rise estates – is that by 1952 Barnett was virtually a lone voice arguing against high-rise public housing. Ironically, the towers were eventually sited on what had once been the very slum pockets he sought to eliminate. Perhaps he sensed that the towers would become part of the problem rather than the solution.

---

1   Barnett, F. O. (1933). The unsuspected slums : an illustrated summary of a thesis submitted to the Melbourne University surveying the slum problem of Melbourne / by F. Oswald Barnett. Melbourne: Herald Press.

The State Library of Victoria holds an extraordinary collection of photographs taken by Barnett and his colleagues – stark, intimate glimpses of the slums and the lives within them. I've returned to those images, arranging them, where possible, into suburban groupings, and including two photographs from rural Victoria that reveal conditions similar to – or worse than – those found in the city at the time. Through this process, I've also journeyed back to the inner-city Melbourne I knew as a nurse in the 1980s, and tried to imagine, as faithfully as I can, what Barnett himself saw in the 1930s. My simple interpretive poetry cannot fully capture the conditions he documented in The Unexpected Slums. Even so, in 2025, it feels timely to try.

Come. Walk with me through *The Unexpected Slums.*

Preface

If you want to know
The truth about the slums
read the illustrated booklet
"**The Unsuspected Slum**"
by F. Oswald Barnett. M.Comm.
Price 1/-
Proceeds in aid of
Methodist Babies' Home

will you (come and listen)

the truth
will cost you
a shilling

just one shilling

that is all
that it costs
to know the truth

will you come along
to listen?

Richmond

Frank Prem

good neighbours (and close)

we rely
on each other

good neighbours

well
you have to be
don't you?

we could lean out
from our verandahs
and meet
in the middle
for a quick
kiss

we're that close

very good neighbours
indeed

up the street (with cricket)

how may fielders?

too many!

not enough!

go call the little-ies
from number four

let's fill the street
up
with cricket

the smell runs down the centre (of loughnan street)

the gutters run
down the centre
of loughnan street

that is
when they choose
to run
at all

we pray
for dry weather

and no rain

so we don't
need to smell
the neighbours
from up the road

a tombstone fence (with pickets)

a picket fence
like broken
gappy tombstones

it doesn't take a lot
to make a home
and
a little fence
has *always*
meant something

it has said
something
about the people
that live inside

anyway
what it says
to me
is that *this* place
is mine

West Melbourne

getting by (in the dudley mansions)

we're a bit
of a shanty town
I suppose

no shops
or anything like that

no money for shops
either
if it comes to it

just a swamp
and
a rubbish tip

we get by
all right

we get by

undeserving (but shop I must)

well
where else
am I going to shop
for materials

to build a home
for me
and mine?

you answer me
that

undeserving poor
is undeserving poor
and that
my dear
is *me*

all I need (and my kookaburra)

welcome
to my humpy home

I made it
myself

not too proud —
you *can't* be proud —
to use things
that I found

my materials

and my kookaburra laughs
like the jackass
that he is

my animals

and me

all I need

WEST MELBOURNE

A "Dudley Mansion". The kitchen is the front room, behind is the bedroom, which is papered with blue bills (salvaged from the tip, the print side being turned inward). No blankets, but cleanly washed bags. The room on the left built for a young man fallen on hard times - so he is lodged free and meals are also given to him by the owner - till recently a sustenance man - the generosity of the poor.

what it is (is hunger)

we don't have much
here in dudley

but a bag
will do
for a blanket

some
are worse
than even me

so I built
a room

he can stay

we all know
what it is
to be hungry

WEST MELBOURNE

One of the "Dudley Mansions". Every thing used in the building has been salvaged from the rubbish tip. The fence is made of wooden slats, scrapped by the Gas Company.

all I needed (a lucky man)

well . . .

it's a funny story . . .

true though

I sort of live
on the rubbish tip
here

and —
you know —
everything . . .

absolutely everything
that is my home
was thrown away
by someone else

waiting
until I found it

a man
can be lucky
I reckon

WEST MELBOURNE

The lavatory to a Dudley Mansion. The day I visited the Mansions the 'lady' told me she could not sleep because of the storm on during the night. "The old shack was all right" she said, "but I was dreadfully afraid of the lavatory."

storm (in a tea-cup) by the water

oh
the storms
can be fierce

we're right by
that bit of backwash
and the outflow
can be fierce

but oh . . .

I don't know
what we would have done
if the wind had got a hold
of the dunny
down by the water

I can tell you
it doesn't bear thinking about
at all

a memory (to take home)

this
is their water supply

over there . . .

a half a mile over that way . . .

are their homes

this
is the mansion life
they live

the mud
on my feet
is
a visitation swamp

and I will carry it —
a memory —
all the way
home

proper buggery (in a storm)

there's always
a brick . . .

or two

but
never any nails

no hammer

most of the time
the roof stays down

stays *on*

it's proper buggery
though
in a storm

Carlton

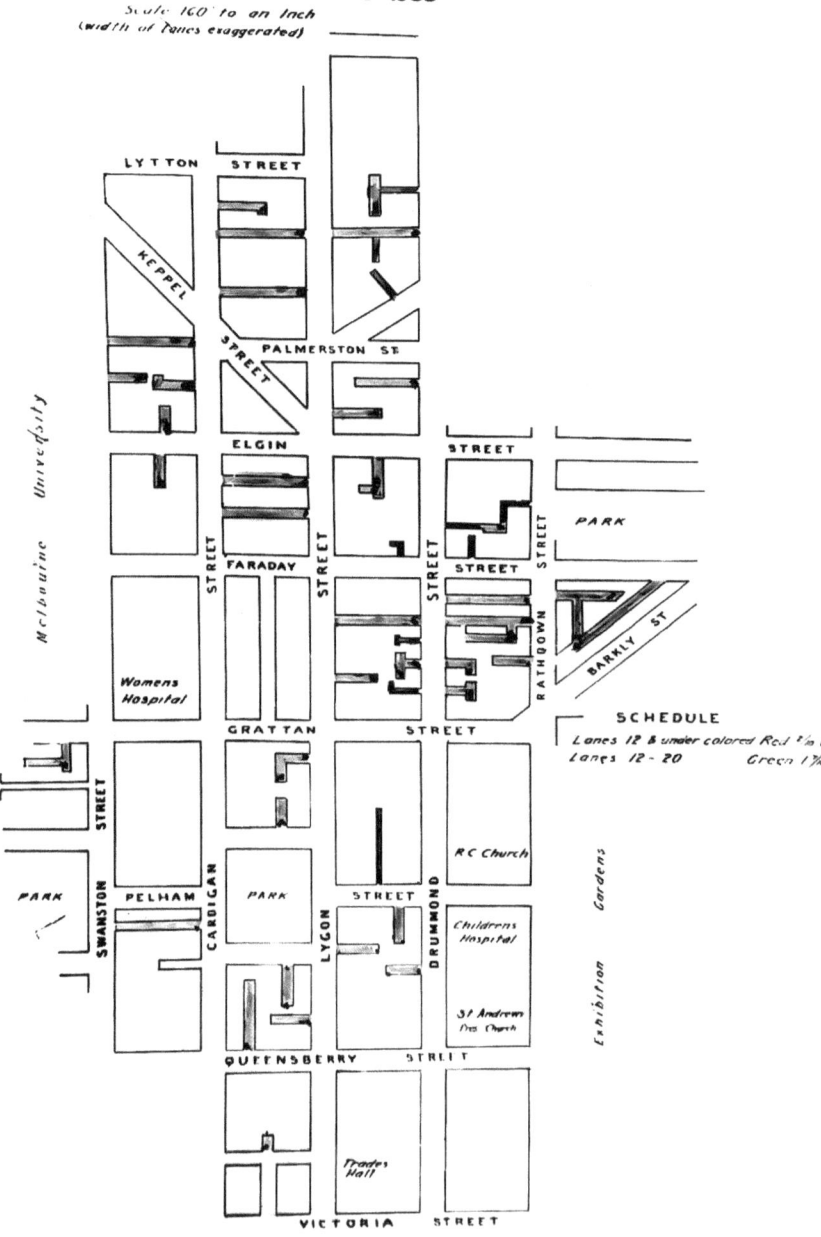

say it (carlton)

seven blocks
from north
to south

four
going across
the other way

I live
in *carlton*

what do you
care

there's nothing
for you
to say

measles that bite (in the night-time)

spots
on their faces

that's all it is

a few spots

might be
the measles . . .

ye-es . . .

it could be that

but
measles don't bite you
in the night-time

while you're sleeping

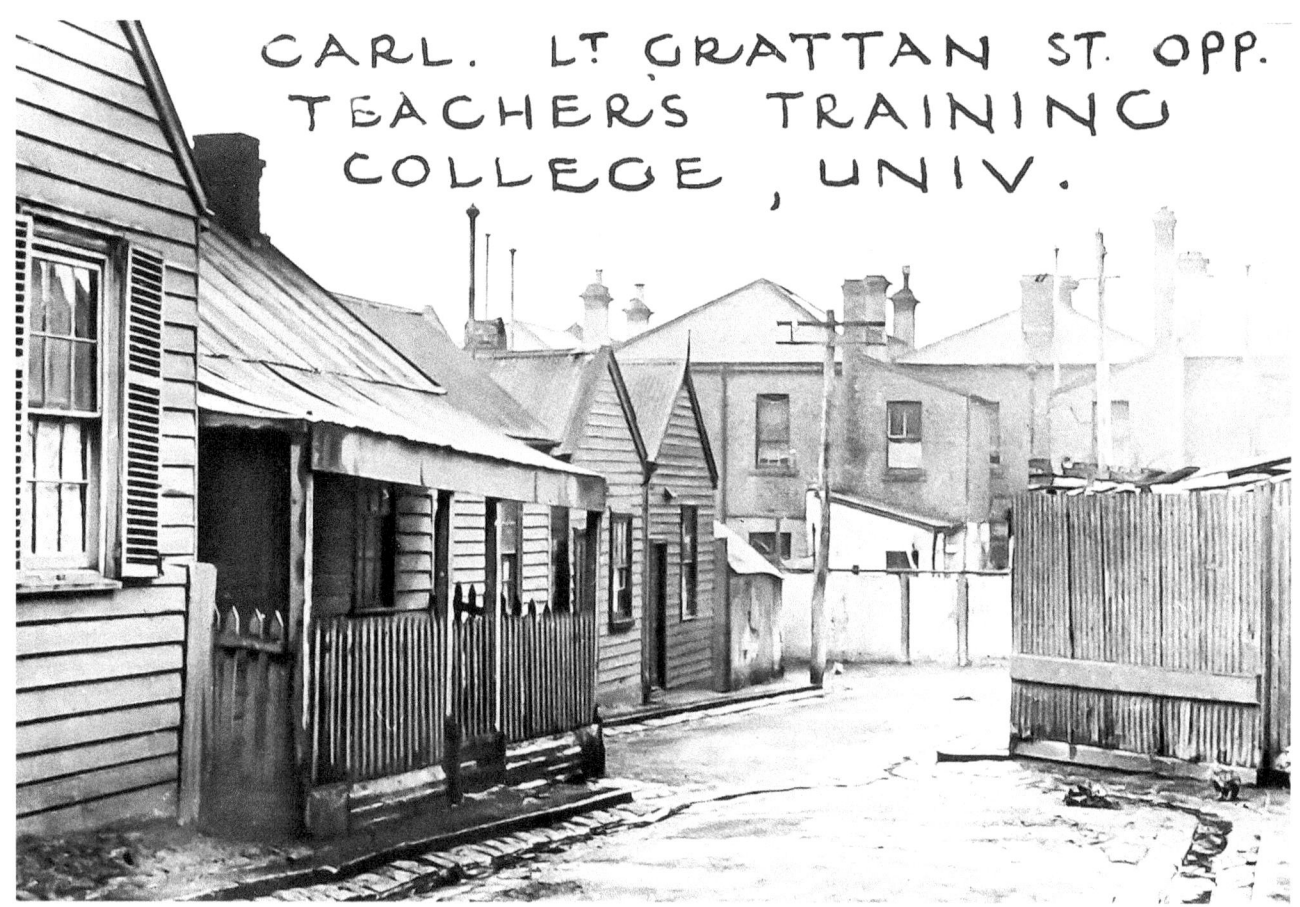

a tumbledown alley (a mostly-dry home)

tumbledown alley

home
right at the seat
of learning

you —
scholar –
what can you learn
from this

what
might you learn
from *me*

a tumbledown alley
that is home

and a roof
to keep out
most of the rain

where else
would I want
to be

Little Barkly Street, Carlton. This house is built on to the rear of an allotment facing Barkly Street.

a shank's pony ride (from little barkly street)

if you look
down there
you'll see
rathdowne street

up the other end
is elgin

you can catch
a tram there
if you can
afford it

then get yourself
around the city

if you can afford it

otherwise
it's shank's pony
for you

and shank's pony
for me

everything (and our children)

we share
everything
in palmerston street

> *our yard*
> *with a dray*
>
> *the alleyway*
> *with a stable*
>
> *our gutters*
> *with filth and muck*

and
our children

our children
we share
with
everything

lucky children (with horses)

there is a horse

and stables

children
do well
when they can be
around animals

when
they can play
around them

right there
in the street
where they live

lucky children

BARKLY ST

FRONT ROOM
12' x 10'

LIVING ROOM
10' x 10'

KITCHEN
6' x 6'

PORCH

YARD

Copper

W.C

W.C

Tap

Bath

YARD

Tap

REAR R'M
10' x 7'

FRONT R'M

3' PASSAGE WAY

BED RM
12' x 10'

BED RM
10' x 10'

UPSTAIRS ROOMS

LAND
13' FRONTAGE
72' DEEP.

1. BATH SERVES TWO HOUSES

1. TAP OVER GULLY TRAP FOR EACH HOUSE

LITTLE BARKLY ST.

sweet sounds (in the backyard)

it's not big enough
to spit across

you'd be spitting
into your neighbour's yard

and you need
to let them know
if you're going to have a bath

you don't want *everyone*
watching
while you wash

you can have
a conversation
though
while you're sitting
on the dunny

the sound of voices
can be a relief
when the usual sound
is thunder

Carlton.
Wash-house and bath-room 48 Palmerston Street. The only water laid on is the tap over the gully trap. The only washing convenience the hand basin on the box. The piece of canvas was erected for the purpose of keeping the wood dry.

shelter wood (from all storms)

you need the wood
dry
because you *have* to have
a fire

it's no good wanting to wash
clothes
or
have a bath
if you've got
no fire

so the wood
has to be covered

protected

but —
god help us —
it still gets wet
when the rain comes down

hard for the weather (to find us)

around a bit . . .

you have to go
around
a bit
to find where we live

but
we're not alone
in there

there's four
of us families
in our four
little cottages

but at least
the weather stops
on the outside

a little less cold (a little more mould)

it's a sort of
roof

with a sort-of
ceiling

we stuff the space
in between
with rags
and clothes too worn out
to be any use

it keeps out
a bit
of the cold

gets pretty mouldy
though

getting by (at a shilling a foot)

they charge us
weekly rent
at about
a shilling a foot
across the width
of this place

eleven shillings
and sixpence
a week

the susso pays less
than that

we get by
somehow

I suppose
we get
by

a nine foot wingspan (would never fit)

I heard tell
that —
not here
but away from the city —
there are big birds

wedge-tailed eagles

they don't fly
but drift around
on hot air
way up high

they're supposed to have
a wingspan
of nine feet across

huh
it couldn't *fly*
or drift around
down here

would never fit
between
the houses

a meal costs a penny (if your dad doesn't work)

dad
doesn't work

none of the dads
have got work

a penny
will buy a meal
if your dad
doesn't work

that's all right (nobody looks)

we don't need
a door
on our dunny

the spiders
and the flies
all get in
anyway

and nobody
looks

so
that's all right

Carlton.
Two Mothers living in house shown in photograph No. 9. Both were under the influence of liquor. The doctor with me, said that one baby had been very ill, and had recovered, but now would die owing to neglect.

no one (nothing)

one child
will live

one child
will die

how are we
to choose

I don't know
who
she might be (no one)

don't know
what
he may become (nothing)

Carlton. Somerset Place. It is stated that there is at least one child in every house in this street who has had diptheria. The condition of the gutter as shown in the photo would tend to support this contention.

home (in the cobblestones)

play
in the gutter
child

splash
the waters high

skip stones
through the filthy street

these cobbles
are home

these
cobblestones
are
your home

cricket and dogs and kids (and hopscotch)

kids
and dogs
on david street

chase their tails
the whole day
long

a cricket pitch
with a bin
and a bat
and a ball

hopscotch
when they find
a small piece
of chalk

almost educated (not likely)

that
is where
the *almost-educated* poor
live

the university is
just around the corner
but
can you imagine . . .

can you just imagine
a university student
or . . .

or a don
coming out of that lot?

no
I can't see it
either

no one (to say boo)

one day
they won't even remember
airedale place

our little blot
on the carlton landscape

they'll look
for us
on a map
and all they'll find
is a little stench

still lingering
from that filthy drain
down there

at the bottleneck

not even a ghost
will stay
to say
boo

no complaints (the walls are thin)

it's a little
tight
living here
in airedale place

it's best
to keep yourself
to yourself

in case
of neighbours

so many neighbours

and the walls . . .

they let the sound through
inside
as though they didn't exist

not that
anyone complains
no

we
don't ever complain

slippy to the lavatory (in the winter)

well
it's not
what you'd call
a *deep* property

only thirteen feet
and we have to hang
the washing out
on the street

but we can get water
from the tap
there
over the gully trap

and
the laundry and bathroom . . .

and the lavatory
are in the shed
at the end
of the lane

it gets a little slippy
in the winter

Collingwood and Abbotsford

I live here (in collingwood)

I am
collingwood

I
live *there* . . .

and *there*

in *abbotsford*

I work in a factory
and
in the brewery

and
I'm on the susso

I am collingwood

here
is where I live

to keep out (of the night)

it's a room

that's more
than some
have got

just one room
but
we are small

we make *it*
do

and we make *us*
fit

one room is enough
to keep out
of the night

little charles we hope for (and bread)

on the street
where *I* live

we pack in
quite
tightly

a little house
in
little charles

that's as much
as anyone
can do . . .

all we
can hope for

and bread

we hope for bread
too
for the table

ooh look (the premier has come)

ooh look

it's the premier
himself
and all his mates

who'd have thought
we'd see the day
down *here*

they don't travel
by themselves
I see

go everywhere
in packs

maybe
they have the right
of that

there's no love
for politicians
in collingwood

an old bag (but it helps)

it's only
a window
and . . .

well
who can afford glass?

not *my* landlord
that's for sure

the wind still blows through
but
there's another bag
on the inside

that helps
a lot

sunshine and fresh air (for the bedding)

the house is a bit
holey
and it lets
the rain in

through the roof
and through
some of the windows
that haven't got glass

every so often
the bedding
gets a bit damp

but
it's a nice day
today

sunshine
and fresh air
will set things
right

whichever way you look (it's a lot of mouths)

the rent
is eight shillings
for
our three rooms

the susso pays
seventeen shillings
and three shillings extra
for each child

nothing over twenty shillings
and sixpence

my husband
will have to work for it too

building parks
and making roads
and such
all by hand

we survive
somehow
but . . .

eight kids is a lot of mouths
to feed
whichever way
you look at it

in and out (like a ginger beer stopper)

well
would you look at them

I don't know
how
they think they'll fit
into number twelve

there's the ten of them
that live there
inside already

they'll be popping out
through the back door
like the stopper
out of a ginger beer
bottle
in a minute

just shut up (and do)

this is where
I wash the clothes

wash myself

where I fetch
the kitchen water

this place
is more than we can pay

more than *anyone*
can pay
on the susso

but
there's six little mouths to feed
as well as us

so we shut up
and do

that's all

shut up
and do

very close (in glasgow street)

we're all
very good neighbours
here

very close

well
you have to be
don't you?

when you can't even
step into the backyard
to pass wind
in private

why
there's *hardly* a backyard
between us

so yes
very close neighbours
we are
in glasgow street

useless in the wet (and a trial through summer)

we haven't got
the room
to swing a cat
out here

so
even the lavy
has to have a second job

propping up
the clothesline

very handy
but
it's a trial
for the smell
in summer

useless
in the wet
through winter

Collingwood.

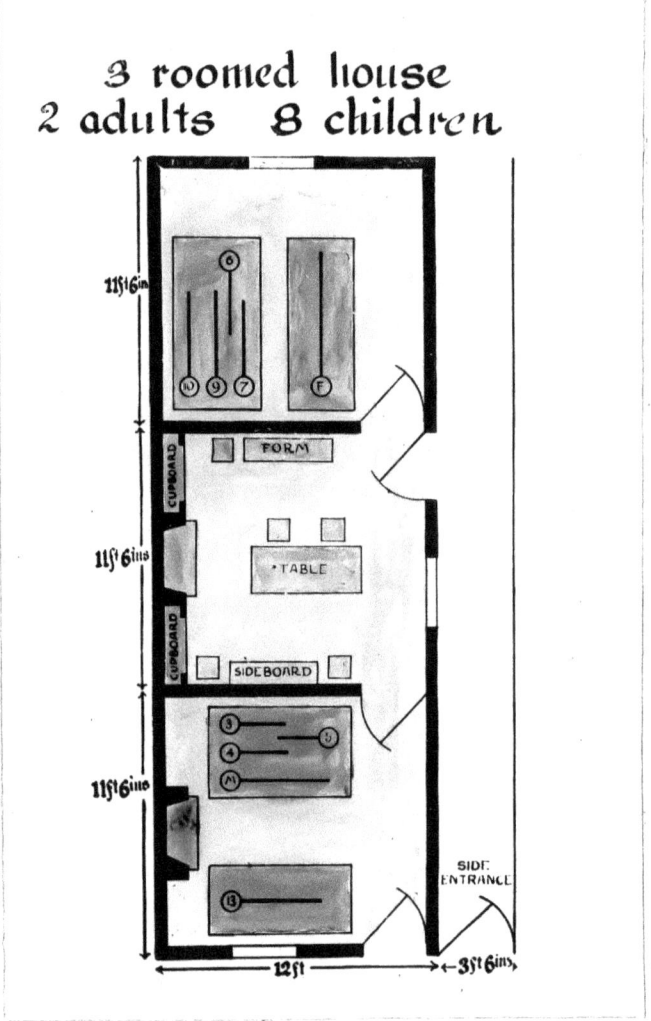

Plan of house No. 12 Hood Street, showing how two adults and eight children can live in a three-roomed house.

what we have to do (top-to-toe)

sleeping them
top-to-toe
is nothing special
around here
in hood street

there's a lot
of kids
in this street
and the cottages
are small

but . . .

nobody minds
really

it's just
what we all
have to do

C'WOOD. OPEN AIR WASH·HOUSE.
· TYPICAL OF THOUSANDS

hell to hang (inside)

you pray
for a fine day

so you can hang the washing
outside

let it dry
in the open air

it's hell —
pardon my language —
when the sun doesn't shine

you still have to wash
but
there's nowhere
to hang it
except inside

high and mighty (in hood street)

lead them
by the nose
and they might
notice you

I wonder
how many of them —
high and mighty's
all of them —

how many
have ever set foot
in hood street
before?

none of them
I bet

not in a window (maybe in a bottle)

glasshouse street?

you'd be lucky
to find *any* glass here
now

maybe once . . .

maybe broken
on the ground . . .

maybe
in the shape
of an empty bottle
of beer

none
in the windows

more damage (as if)

careful there . . .

be careful
where you step

the landlord
won't have us
doing any more damage
to the fittings

as if
we could

hessian and paper (none at all)

rokeby
is all right

I mean
really . . .

some of the streets
around here —
waterloo
and glasshouse
for instance —

are shockers

hessian and paper

might as well
have no wall
between the houses
at all

bail the bath (and seal the door)

they charge us
for three rooms
and a bathroom

we have to supply
our own bailer
to empty the bath
though

the drain is blocked

and one of the rooms . . .

well
you can't
go in there

we try to —
sort of —
seal it off
from the rest
of the house

there's just too many
bugs

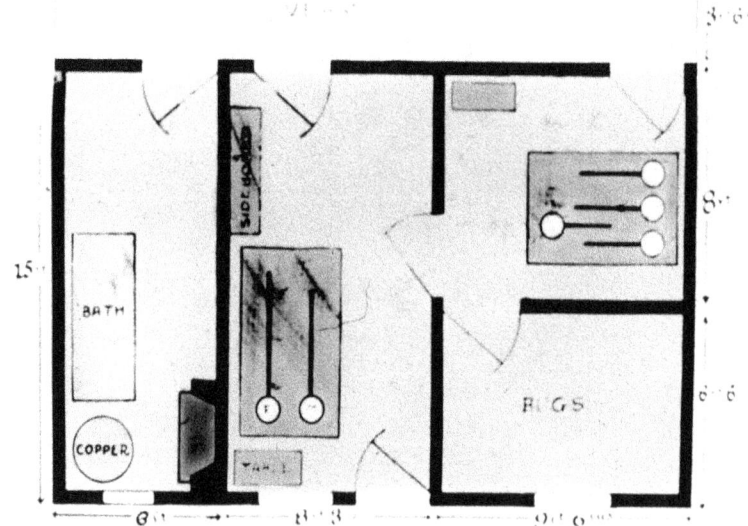

the best we can (or eaten alive)

the kitchen
is out the back

there's no washhouse
so we have to do
the best we can
there

and we can only —
really —
use two rooms
in the house
for sleeping
and
the bathroom

that third bedroom
we just can't use

you get eaten alive
in there

packed in (a good proposition)

eight shillings
and sixpence
for a house
made out of packing case wood

still
it's a roof
over our heads
isn't it?

there's times
when that seems
like a very good proposition
indeed

it takes all the air (to breathe)

my husband
and seven

that's what we are
and
what we've got

it's crushing in there
sometimes

like
just living
has stolen away
all the air there is
in the world
to breathe

not proud (but our best)

our front yard
is a drain

you can't be proud
of that
but . . .

we raise our kids
as well
as we might

feed them

find clothes
for them

send them
to the school

we do
our best

for something better (but they don't mind)

bluestone
gets slippery
when it's wet

it's a treacherous journey
just to get
to the street

and
to the shops

there's filth too
sometimes

the kids don't seem
to mind it
much

but . . .

once upon a time
I might have hoped
for something better
for them

Fitzroy

Fitzroy Town Hall. In reply to the request of the Government, Fitzroy replied it had no slums.

no I repeat no (slums in fitzroy)

just
to be clear . . .

before you start

you need to know
that —
no matter what
you think
you see —

there are no slums —
I'll repeat that —
there are no
slums
in fitzroy

the beating heart (a place of pride)

it is
a beautiful place
fitzroy

wide thoroughfares . . .

victoria parade . . .

our municipality
is rightly proud
of its place
at the beating heart
of melbourne

alive and dead (outside their doors)

grand
isn't it?

fitzroy
has always taken itself
seriously

the people
that go in
and out
of that grand place there . . .

the town hall

they don't know
what's alive
and
what's dead
in their own
streets

just outside
their own doors

no point complaining (no one will listen)

well there's —
sort of —
ten rooms for us
to squeeze into

some downstairs and
some upstairs

and some sleep-outs
at the back

half a dozen men
half a dozen
women

a full dozen of children
running around
and all over
the place

we do ok
though

can't complain

there's nobody to listen

something chronic (the key's not out)

you ought to hear
the row
when someone
gets locked out

usually
they'll have had too much
to drink
and they'll carry on
something chronic
if the key's not there
for them

it might be funny
if you weren't
trying to get a bit
of blessed sleep

there's no kitchens (if you're on the susso)

nine rooms
at five bob a week
each . . .

that's over two pound
a week for the house

and
a penny in the slot
to get the gas flowing
so you can cook
in the kitchen
but
nobody does that

can't afford it

we all cook
in our own rooms
in the fireplace
or
in a kerosene tin

you can't afford kitchens
if you're living
on the susso

chicken wire (to feel safer in the night)

this has always
been
a rough area

back a few years
they called this
vendetta street
and
the gang feuding
was fierce

some woman
got shot in the head
by the villains
and thieves
that were fighting
among themselves

a lot of people
put up chicken wire
on the windows
and other barricades

to try to feel
a bit safer
in the night

push and push back (it was war in little napier)

it was
a proper war
around here

back in the 1920s it was

and the richmond push
and the fitzroy push
were at each other

they were all
a bunch of thugs
and it seemed like
the great war in europe
taught them how to fight
dirty

to use guns
at the drop of a hat

barbed wire
on the fence . . .

that
was the least
of it

Fitzroy.
Little George Street, Fitzroy. The woman in the picture was intoxicated by Fitzroy's famous "rot gut" wine.

the very devil (that leaves you numbed)

rot gut

it's a pretty rough drop
for sure

leaves you standing . . .

but
only if you've got
something
to lean on . . .

it leaves you
standing in a stupor

like you've got a shivering
numb chill
all over

burns
your throat
like the very devil

it *is*
the very devil

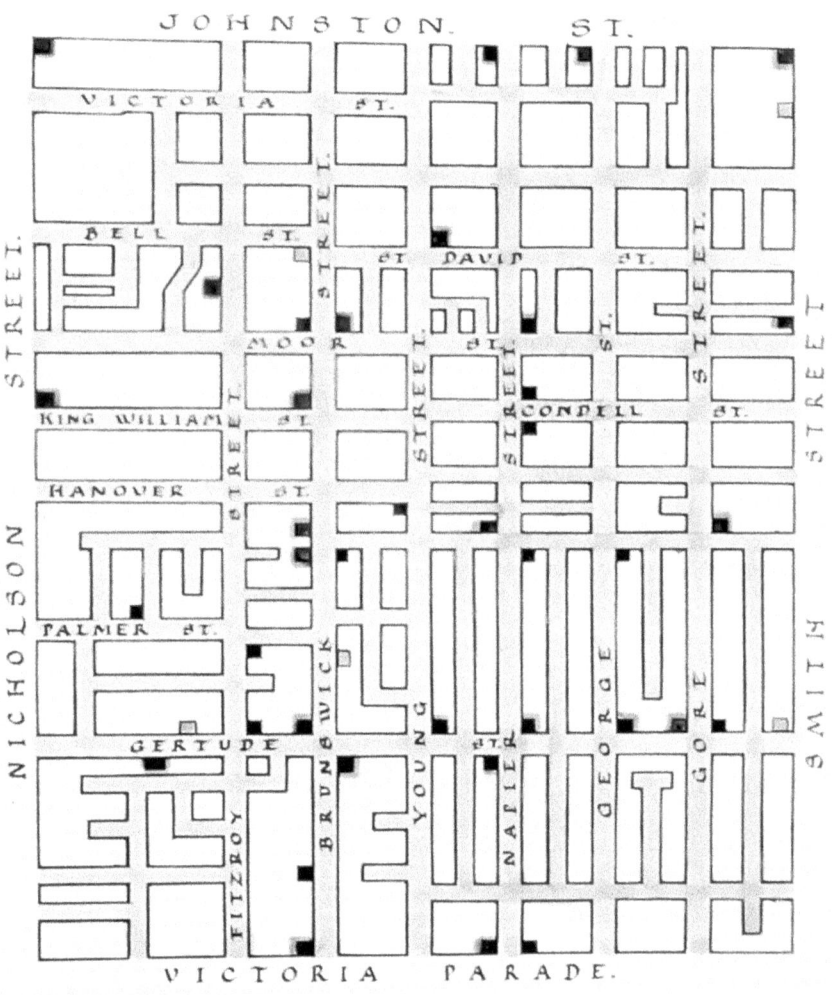

almost enough rotgut (and close-by to boot)

they say
we drink a lot
here in *the 'roy*

and
I suppose
that we do

what else
can you do

with no work
and leaking roofs
and snot-nosed children
running around you
all the long day?

a little rotgut
from a convenient location . . .

that
is *almost* enough
to help you
get by

Fitzroy.
View from the Brotherhood of St. Lawrence, showing the rear of four pairs of cottages "one in process of disappearing". No bathrooms, so tenants wash in the open.

god and the brotherhood and the rain (to watch over us)

god
and the brotherhood
and
the salvo's
watch over us

saints
of the world
that have to watch
while we wash
our clothes
and our children
and
ourselves

all in the wide open
with the sound of rain
on the roof
behind
to sing
about the foolish life
that we lead

a place for the kiddies (to play)

don't you know
what it is?

silly!
it's playground

for the kiddies

it's lovely
for the little tikes
to have a place
to go

to play

a place to play (if you know what I mean)

it's not always
nice
for the little ones
at home

you know
mother or father
might be having a drink
or such

sometimes
it's better
if the kiddies
take themselves away
so it's good
that there's a place
they can come
to play

not far from home
but
not in anyone's road
either

if you know
what I mean

a place (in the fitzroy night)

some high
lord mucky muck
owns it
they reckon

it's so bad
that even he
won't rent it out

still . . .

there's many
that have got no
other place
and no
other choice

so
they'll sneak
a bit of straw in

to have a place
to lie down
in the night

alone we die (in marion street)

we die quiet . . .

    alone

in marion street

for
there is no room —
besides the dying —
to mourn

there's hardly the *room* —
in marion street —
to take a last breath

hardly the room —
at the end
of your days —
to die

it'll do (until something better)

don't say
it's not much

and don't tell me
it isn't enough

I know all that

we watch the damp
rise
and we catch
the drips
every time it rains

but
it's a roof
and
we all squeeze in

that'll do
until you've got
something better
for us

ten to her the rest to me (and the metho)

the bungalows
are all right

the metho
doesn't allow
for much more

and the landlady . . .

she helps us
out

takes us
to collect the pension
every two weeks

ten shillings each
goes straight
to her

the rest
to live on . . .

and
another drop
of metho

tin is cold (so we do what we must)

some of us
live
in wood
and bricks

some of us
live in tin

a house
is a house
but tin
is cold

so I buy
and I sell —
this and that —
on the sly

to keep warm

we all do
what we must
to keep ourselves warm

three by three no bathroom (in argyle street)

three houses
with three rooms
in argyle street

each room
nine feet by nine . . .

that's
two hundred
and forty-three feet
per family

ten shillings
and sixpence
per week

no bathroom

ten and six
won't get you
a bathroom
in argyle street

it's all right (if you can't see the damp)

they look really solid
buildings

all fine brickwork
and quality finish

but inside . . .

the damp
is so bad
we have to nail up the ceiling
to keep it
from falling down
on top of us

anyway
you can hardly see
the damp
because there's no light
to speak of
inside

so
that's all right

North Melbourne

the sun shines somewhere (not here)

you don't need
to see the sun
to know
where it is . . .

that it shines down
every day

that's
what the landlord tells us

I suppose
that it must be true

away down the alley
and
out there
on the street
at least

lord knows
it doesn't shine
here

North Melbourne.
Hardwicke Street. Dilapidated houses Rusty roofs. City Council has proposed rebuilding of this area. The first scheme was cottages. Each cottage, with land to cost £1375. That scheme was abandoned and the present scheme under discussion is one of tenement buildings.

hardwicke street (tenements up into the sky)

it's just
a tumble-down old street
with nothing
to recommend it
really

runs along between
molesworth
at one end
and haines
at the other

so yes

it's worth pushing down
and not a lot
else

but
it's all *we've* ever known

and it can't be right
for people to live
three floors up

in the sky

accordion (enough)

it isn't
what I want
but
this is what I get

I can hear the rainfall
in the nighttime

and the sun
sings songs
through the walls
and the roof

accordion contractions
and clangs

it's enough

it has to be
enough

rats (that come a-calling)

there are rats
in the walls
and
there are rats
beneath the floor

rats
that come
a-calling

a bunch
of rats
outside
my door

just like that (bastard)

there was
two of them

a mum
and her boy

they're not there
any more

not sure
where
they've gone to live
now

evicted —
just like *that* —
by the landlord

bastard

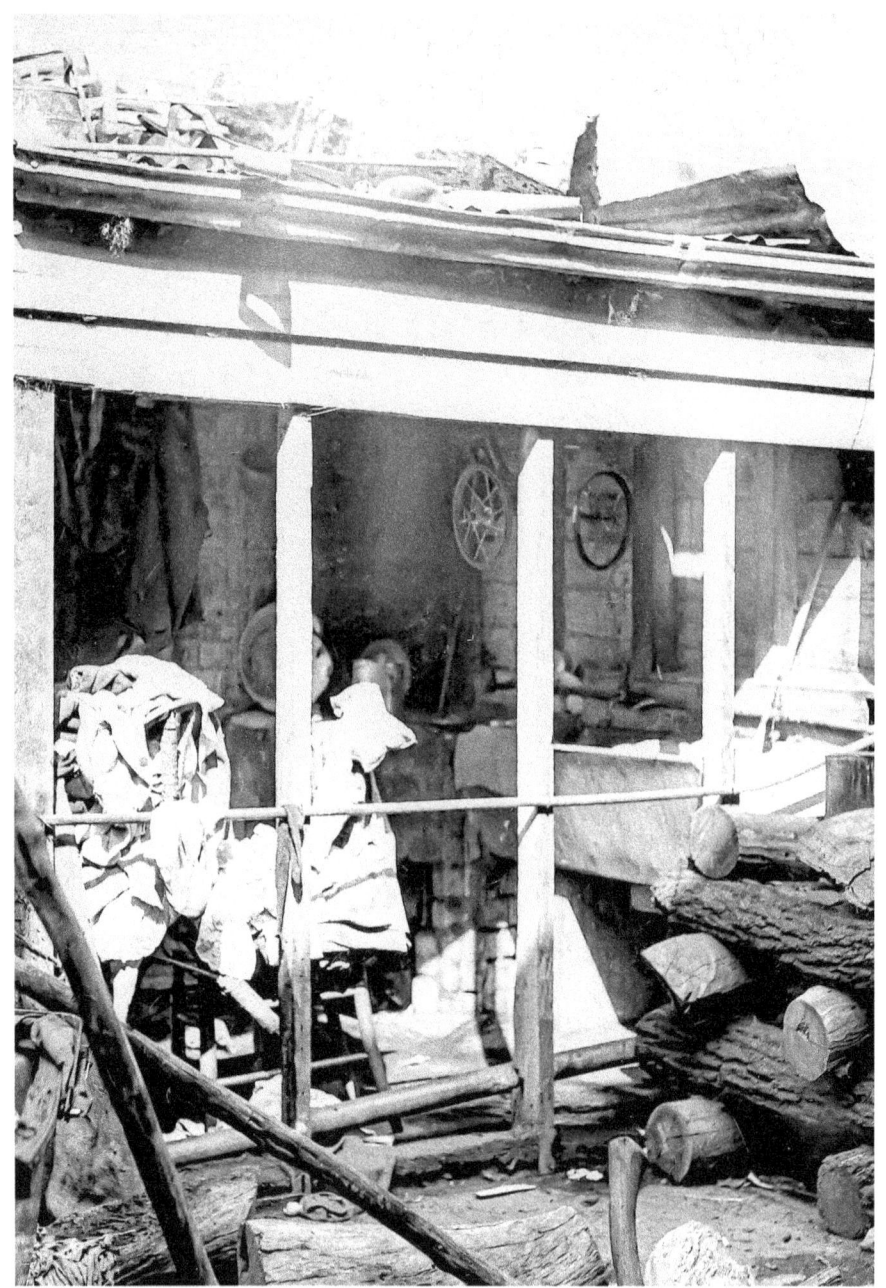

ah well (the trough's under cover)

it's a bit
of a jumble
but this
is the washhouse

the trough
is under cover
although
the roof leaks

there's rubbish everywhere
really

even
up on the roof

ah well

there are worse (we survive)

it's true

the holes
do
let the rain in

and there's nowhere
outside
to dry the wash

it's true
we don't like
living
this way

and
we're all packed in
like sardines
but . . .

there are worse
off
than us

we survive

quiet sunshine (ten minutes a day)

around the corner
then
around the corner
again

   two in

   two up

that's us

we get
our ten minutes
of sunshine —
if it isn't cloudy
or raining —
every day

it comes in
through the side door

it's a nice
quiet
little street
is ours

damp enough (to make you sick)

damp?

well
we've got it
chronic

and mould

it's enough
to make you
sick

it means nothing (when it has always been)

well
I don't know
if it's disgusting
or not

I've never
known any different

this is just where we live
and how we live

the drains
run under the house . . .

and there's no light
unless we open
the front door . . .

so what?

it doesn't *mean* anything

not when you've
always
lived like this

to the copper (all the money went)

copper's got
a hole in it

add sixpence
to the rent

copper's got a hole
in it

that's where
the money
went

don't try to deal
with the landlord

he's got
a heart
of flint

the copper
has got
a hole in it
and that's where
all the money
went

the rat goes on (forever)

come on inside
the water
is just on the boil

excuse
where I've been sweeping
but
the rat
that resides there
is sometimes
a bit messy
and . . .

you know

the cleaning
just goes

on and on
forever
it goes

NORTH MELB. HIS ONLY BATHROOM ON A COLD & FROSTY MORNING

it's no good (half asleep)

well
it's a face
that needs washing
you know

it's not very pretty
when it's left
to its own
devices
and looks

the water's cold
and
guaranteed
to wake you

but there's no good
will come
from starting a day
half asleep

we will survive (baby mine)

baby mine
I will save the pennies
that the government
gives

to see you born

you and I . . .

we're alone
but we can buy
food

I will
survive

you
will have food

tin (not gingerbread)

you've heard —
I suppose —
of a house made
out of gingerbread?

well
this one is made
from rusty tin

from holey tin

and the rain
comes down
while the wind
whistles through

it creaks
and it groans
and
we all creak
and groan

that's life isn't it?

tin
not gingerbread

no room so (that's fair)

the oldest
is responsible
for the rest

that's fair

the way
it's always been

there's no room
for them to play
at home
so . . .

they have to be
outside

the oldest
is responsible

it's fair

there are some (with gutter)

there's houses
around the corner . . .

they're no wider
than this
poor
pathetic
right-of-way

nine foot
of house front . . .

just a man
and a half
across

some of them
with the gutter running
underneath them
as well

mind your own (and draw the awning down)

even if
the house had windows

still we'd keep
the awning down

there is no cause
for anyone
else
to mind
our business

bad dreams (are dreamt in twilight)

I dream
in the daytime
inside

it is always evening
in there

always as though
the sun
has set

I can forget that
it's bright sunshine
outside

and can't remember
what time it is
in the half-light
and half-dark
of this place

I have no life
that is not a bad dream
dreamt
in twilight

higgle and piggle (in north melbourne)

the fence between
is like
a row
of rotten teeth

or dilapidated gravestones
all higgledy
and piggledy
around a cemetery

that's us

higgledy and piggledy
all over
north melbourne

South and Port Melbourne

a house (yes it is)

yes

it's a house

what
did you think
it would be?

at fifteen bob a week
it had *better* be
a house

it's only a shame
that
it isn't a darn sight
better
for *that* money

not on your shoes (or legs)

be careful
where you walk

place your feet
only
where you see
stone

sometimes
the lane is foul
so
try not to get
the spatter
on your shoes
or
your legs

washing day (kids out clothes in)

washing day

the tub
that serves as our bath
becomes
the copper

doesn't matter

clothes go in

clothes come out

the fire
makes the water
just as hot for the one
as it does
for another

where else? (right there)

you wouldn't call it
living . . .

no

I don't suppose
anyone
would call it
that

but still . . .

people
have got to be
somewhere

and —
I ask you —
where else
have they got
to go?

more or less (it is whole)

they fall
to the ground
from time
to time

weatherboards
or
sheets of fencing

get on the scrounge
and you can find
a nail . . .

borrow
a hammer

somehow
keep the whole thing —
more or less —
whole

still like convicts (more or less)

they say
the first convicts
came
to the first prison —
here
in australia —
wearing chains

I wonder
what would they say
all these years
later

if they knew
that we live —
more
or less —
in irons
now

singing (like you're dying)

you get used
to the sound

a house like this —
and
all its neighbours
too —
is never quiet

daytime
or night-time

it makes no difference

on good days
it's a little bit
like
a song

bad days
you can feel like
you're dying

Other Places Other Slums

up and down (a little love goes)

little dolls
held by
little dolls

the love
goes up
and down

and we do
the best
we can

a little dirt

a little
wear . . .

that
doesn't matter

nothing matters
but the love

a straitened alley (a straitened supper)

an alley
of iron laces
on wooden frames

chimneys
in solemn lines
of dignity

people live
their lives
constrained

and straitened

but
children play
on the cobbles

in the afternoon
when school
is done

play
and wait
for supper

a whistle (through the hessian)

don't let the wind
catch you
when it whistles
through
the hessian

a double layer
on the bedroom wall
won't keep you
warm

and a thin dress
in the kitchen
is a shiver
with the breakfast
gruel

so don't let
the wind catch you
in the hessian

bloody eyesore (to live in)

push the bastard
over
or
let it burn
perhaps

it wasn't much
standing
but
it's even less
now it's gone

a bloody eyesore

useless
to live in

pretty (the sty)

a pretty paper
to cover the sty

pretty once
maybe

but
a sty
always

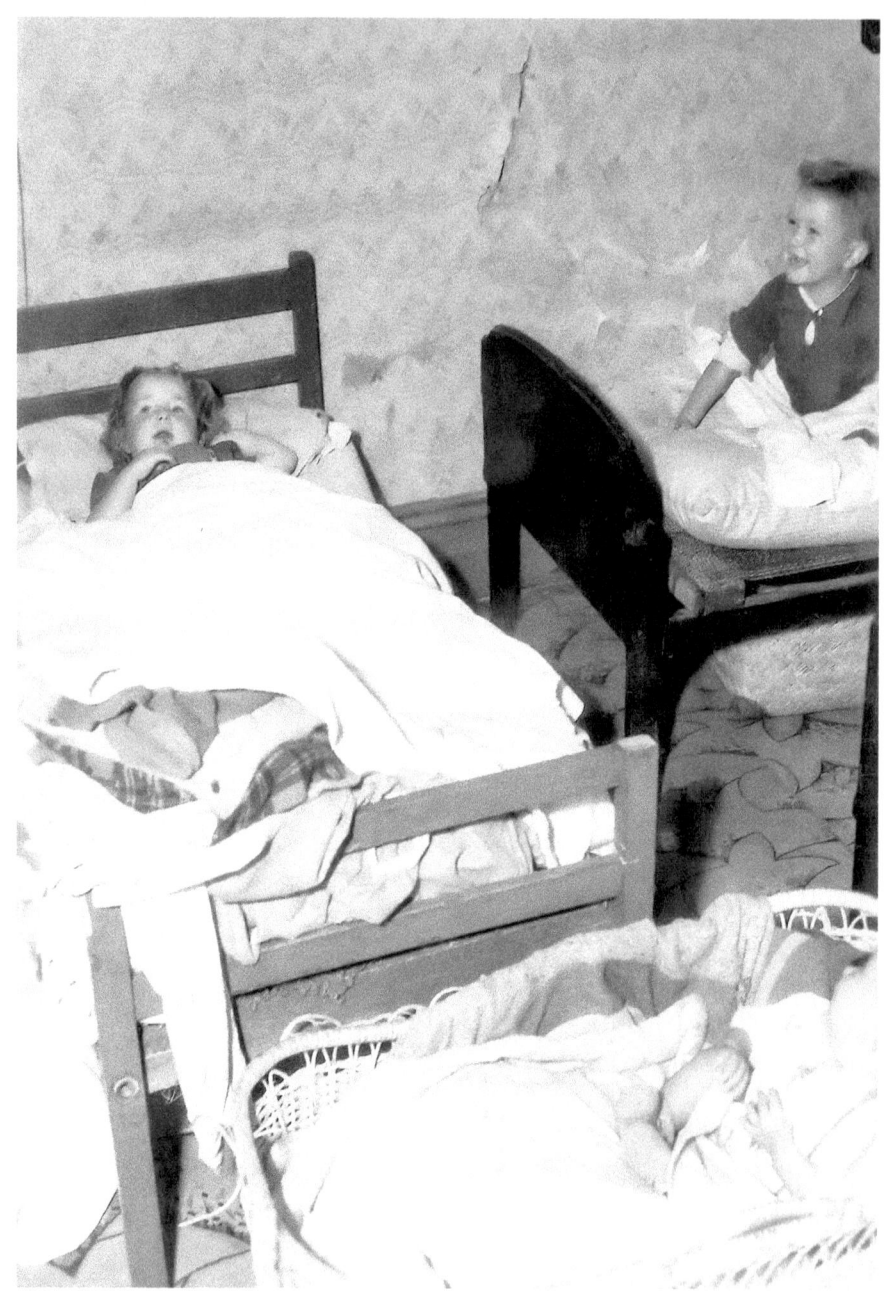

a lullaby (of no harm tonight)

who will sing
a lullaby
for little ones
to sleep?

go to sleep
little ones

be safe
in your beds

no harm will come
through the cracks
in the walls
tonight

so go to sleep
be safe
tonight
little ones

but (we couldn't anyway)

they need to build
a bigger table

we
could certainly use one
but . . .

there's always a *but*
isn't there?

but
we couldn't afford
to buy it
anyway

shabby (is the gift)

shabby gifts
from
a shabby santa
but . . .

this
is where the joy
lies

thank god
there are a few
shabby
little things
that still count
as gifts

from where they live (they're all vermin)

rats and mice

vermin

people

ha ha

how
can you tell
which one
is which . . .

just going by
where
they live . . .

how can you tell?

worth something (a little)

it's as neat
as a pin

a woman
can get her work done —
her washing
and such —
in a clean washhouse

that's worth
something
I reckon

at least
a little
something

ho ho ho (for little children)

ho ho ho

merry christmas
to everyone

ho ho ho
little children

ho
ho
ho

we can be clean (at least)

at *least* we've got
wood
for the copper

and somewhere
out of the rain
to hang a shirt
to dry

at *least*
we can be
clean

6 Lit Charles St
Abbotsford
Tuesday 5

Mr Barnett.
Dear Sir.

I was rather impressed with your lecture & slides which I attended in Wesley Church last Friday night. One thing puzzled me & would be pleased to know if the first street you showed was the above street where you said Maune Yard was in street also J.B. car on verandah. This street I live in is a disgrace. The footpath is all broken & piece of tin sticking up & hole in road & dye runs over footpath from factory into this hole & odor at times is awful. I have a decent house but right along side of children's bedroom windows is stables & the yard is full of rubbish. Certain times of the day Maune carts are on the footpath & it is impossible to come out the gate. to go messages. One Councillor told me if I wanted footpath repaired I would have to pay for same. Wishing you every success

the hole is an odour (I'll have to fix myself)

the footpath —
this my street
I'm talking about —
is a disgrace

there are holes
with tin
sticking out of them

and dye
from the factory
spills over
and into the holes

the odour
is awful

apparently
if I want to fix
anything
I'll have to pay for it
myself

a hot bath (feed the heater)

well
at least it's inside

and I can have
a hot bath

as long as I can feed
the heater

a good man (look at the camera)

now
just you stand
there
on the other side
of the drain
and look at the camera

mister barnett
wants to take
your picture

he's a good man
so you
just do
what he's asking you
to

he's
a good man

right at the door (marvelous)

well
the factory
is just there

right outside
the front door

it would be
a marvellous thing
if they ever had work
for the likes
of us . . .

of *me*

love your neighbour (keep no secrets)

make sure
you can love your neighbour
in our street

you almost
have to
we're so close

a good thing
I've never had
a secret
worth the keeping

not
around here

waste not (on temporary measures)

well
they're just boys
aren't they?

still growing

what good
is a pair of shoes
to the likes
of them?

no point
wasting the little
that we've got
on such temporary
measures

not quite (like the parliament)

they're not
the standard . . .

not *quite*
the same standard
as you find
in the parliament
house

are they
mister premier?

not quite
like that
at all

life in a doll house (of some sort anyway)

it's like a little doll house
isn't it

tacked onto a factory wall

only
we're not dolls

we're people

our children
have to grow up here
with the noise
and the smell
and nowhere to play
but the factory gates

that's life
I suppose

some sort
of life
anyway

my bible and god (first)

you know I have
my pictures

and my prayers
all around me
in their frames

on my walls

the bible
is my companion

my bible
and
my prayers

and god

company (at mealtimes)

six houses
in the street

six small mouths
at the table

and adults
of course

we don't lack for company
at mealtimes

no trouble (do they)

the children
don't take
to strangers

no more than me
or their dad
are like to do

strangers are . . .

well

no one likes trouble
coming up
to their door
do they?

no harm (walk to school)

it's very handy
having the street
in front
and being so close
to the corner

with the vacant lot
next door
there's somewhere
for the kids
to amuse themselves

and just around the corner
the school
isn't far

it does them
no harm
to walk to school
by themselves

there's no harm
in that

SHEPPARTON.

whatever and wherever (a tin house)

you have to
collect
all the tin

from all sorts
of miles
around

rubbish tips and dumps

old sheds and houses . . .

whatever . . .

wherever

then —
if you can
still remember
what they *look* like —
you can build
for yourself
a nice little house

surprisingly good (for a sieve)

well
it's *surprisingly* good
is hessian

up to a point
mind you . . .

only
up to a point

when it rains —
serious-like —
a bloody old roof
made
out of hessian
will leak
like a sieve

quite cosy (really)

it's not a lot
to look at
but . . .

I can cook
on the gas
when there is food
for it

and it's
a cosy little place

really
it's quite cosy

Conclusion

saddle up (it's the same again)

well
we end the same way
as we began

it's always been like that
don't you know?

never mind

saddle up —
why don't you —
and
give it another go

After Words

Image Sources

All images used in this book were sourced under creative commons or otherwise out of copyright. The majority have been sourced from the State Library of Victoria (SLV)Attribution has been given, below.

Behind the Scenes

>**Image Credit:** *Barnett, F. Oswald. 1935. State Library of Victoria. [Behind the scenes]*
>**Image URL:** *https://find.slv.vic.gov.au/permalink/61SLV_INST/1sev8ar/alma9917776253607636*
>**F. Oswald Barnett's Notes:** *Printed u.r.: By courtesy of "The Herald." Printed l.r.: Gurney.*
>**Image Description:** *City of Melbourne image shows a boat on the river with tree-lined banks and the city skyline above; slum image beneath reveals high-density housing.*

will you (come and listen)

>**Image Credit:** *Barnett, F. Oswald. 1935. State Library of Victoria. [Advertisement for the booklet The Unsuspected Slum]*
>**Image URL:** *https://find.slv.vic.gov.au/permalink/61SLV_INST/1sev8ar/alma9917776233607636*
>**F. Oswald Barnett's Notes:**
>**Image Description:** *Promotional text urging readers to learn "the truth about the slums" in the illustrated booklet The Unsuspected Slum by F. F. Oswald Barnett. Proceeds in aid of the Methodist Babies' Home.*

good neighbours (and close)

>**Image Credit:** *Barnett, F. Oswald. 1935. State Library of Victoria. [Street view]*
>**Image URL:** *https://find.slv.vic.gov.au/permalink/61SLV_INST/1sev8ar/alma9917777473607636*
>**F. Oswald Barnett's Notes:**
>**Image Description:** *View down a narrow bluestone-paved street with brick walls in the foreground and small houses and a brick wall at the far end.*

up the street (with cricket)

>**Image Credit:** *Barnett, F. Oswald. 1935. State Library of Victoria. [Children playing cricket]*
>**Image URL:** *https://find.slv.vic.gov.au/permalink/61SLV_INST/1sev8ar/alma9917775473607636*
>**F. Oswald Barnett's Notes:** *Early 30's.*
>**Image Description:** *Children playing cricket in a narrow street bordered by small weatherboard houses. Parked cars visible in the background.*

the smell runs down the centre (of loughnan street)

    Image Credit: *Barnett, F. Oswald. 1935. State Library of Victoria. [Richmond. Loughnan St.]*
    Image URL: *https://find.slv.vic.gov.au/permalink/61SLV_INST/1sev8ar/alma9917775543607636*
    F. Oswald Barnett's Notes:
    Image Description: *Narrow street lined with small weatherboard houses with picket fences. A parked car is partly visible in the background.*

a tombstone fence (with pickets)

    Image Credit: *Barnett, F. Oswald. 1935. State Library of Victoria. [Richmond. Victoria Pl.]*
    Image URL: *https://find.slv.vic.gov.au/permalink/61SLV_INST/1sev8ar/alma9917775513607636*
    F. Oswald Barnett's Notes: *Rich. Victoria pl. 2 storey wooden.*
    Image Description: *Close-up rear (or side) view of a row of double-storey weatherboard houses with a wooden picket fence in front.*

getting by (in the dudley mansions)

    Image Credit: *Barnett, F. Oswald. 1935. State Library of Victoria. [West Melbourne. Dudley Mansions]*
    Image URL: *https://find.slv.vic.gov.au/permalink/61SLV_INST/1sev8ar/alma9917773753607636*
    F. Oswald Barnett's Notes: *West Melb. Swamp. Made from rubbish tip.*
    Image Description: *View across a hillside and stretch of water to a group of shanties, with an industrial landscape in the background.*

undeserving (but shop I must)

    Image Credit: *Barnett, F. Oswald. 1935. State Library of Victoria. [West Melbourne rubbish tip]*
    Image URL: *https://find.slv.vic.gov.au/permalink/61SLV_INST/1sev8ar/alma9917773733607636*
    F. Oswald Barnett's Notes: *West Melbourne rubbish tip from which unemployed people gather pieces of galvanised iron, old tanks, old iron bedstead frames and other material used to build houses nicknamed the Dudley Mansions. On the skyline at left can be seen some men picking over the rubbish.*
    Image Description: *Open area strewn with rubbish. Three figures visible on the horizon.*

all I need (and my kookaburra)

Image Credit: Barnett, F. Oswald. 1935. State Library of Victoria. [West Melbourne. The front view of a "Dudley Mansion."]
Image URL: https://find.slv.vic.gov.au/permalink/61SLV_INST/17t49l2/alma9917773743607636
F. Oswald Barnett's Notes: West Melbourne. The front view of a "Dudley Mansion." The chimney is made from an old circular tank. The kookaburra perched upon it is made out of wood. The chimney top is decorated by a poster advertising Eta peanut butter. The front fence is made from discarded bedsteads; side fences are of brushwood.
Image Description: Front view of a house constructed from discarded materials, surrounded by a fence of metal poles and brushwood. Two dogs and a cat inside the fence; one dog outside.

what it is (is hunger)

Image Credit: Barnett, F. Oswald. 1935. State Library of Victoria. [West Melbourne. A "Dudley Mansion."]
Image URL: https://find.slv.vic.gov.au/permalink/61SLV_INST/1sev8ar/alma9917773783607636
F. Oswald Barnett's Notes: West Melbourne. A "Dudley Mansion." The kitchen is the front room; behind it is the bedroom, papered with blue bills salvaged from the tip with the print side turned inward. No blankets, but cleanly washed bags. The room on the left was built for a young man fallen on hard times — he is lodged free and meals are also given to him by the owner.
Image Description: Front view of a house constructed from discarded materials, surrounded by a fence made from metal poles and brushwood.

all I needed (a lucky man)

Image Credit: Barnett, F. Oswald. 1935. State Library of Victoria. [West Melbourne. A "Dudley Mansion."]
Image URL: https://find.slv.vic.gov.au/permalink/61SLV_INST/1sev8ar/alma9917773873607636
F. Oswald Barnett's Notes: West Melbourne. One of the Dudley Mansions. Everything used in the building has been salvaged from the rubbish tip. The fence is made of wooden slats scrapped by the Gas Company.
Image Description: View of a shanty in an open grassy area with a wooden fence along the left-hand side and industrial buildings in the background.

storm (in a tea-cup) by the water

Image Credit: Barnett, F. Oswald. 1935. State Library of Victoria. [West Melbourne. The lavatory to a Dudley Mansion.]
Image URL: https://find.slv.vic.gov.au/permalink/61SLV_INST/1sev8ar/alma9917773943607636
F. Oswald Barnett's Notes: West Melbourne. The lavatory to a Dudley Mansion. The day I visited the Mansions the "lady" told me she could not sleep because of the storm during the night: "The old shack was all right," she said, "but I was dreadfully afraid of the lavatory."
Image Description: Poorly constructed lavatory building on the edge of a stretch of water, mainly corrugated iron. A rail freight car and industrial landscape are visible in the background.

a memory (to take home)

Image Credit: Barnett, F. Oswald. 1935. State Library of Victoria. [West Melbourne. The stand pipe.]
Image URL: https://find.slv.vic.gov.au/permalink/61SLV_INST/1sev8ar/alma9917773723607636
F. Oswald Barnett's Notes: —
Image Description: Man in a bowler hat and overcoat standing next to a water hydrant in a large open area; water visible on the ground and an industrial landscape in the background.

proper buggery (in a storm)

Image Credit: Barnett, F. Oswald. 1935. State Library of Victoria. [West Melbourne. The rear view of one of the "Dudley Mansions."]
Image URL: https://find.slv.vic.gov.au/permalink/61SLV_INST/1sev8ar/alma9917773833607636
F. Oswald Barnett's Notes: —
Image Description: Rear view of a shanty in an open grassy area constructed from discarded materials; rail freight cars and an industrial landscape are visible in the background.

say it (carlton)

Image Credit: Barnett, F. Oswald. 1935. State Library of Victoria. [Carlton, showing residential lanes, 1935]
Image URL: https://find.slv.vic.gov.au/permalink/61SLV_INST/1sev8ar/alma9917774033607636
F. Oswald Barnett's Notes:
Image Description: Hand-coloured map, dated 1935, showing residential lanes in Carlton bordered by Victoria Street, Exhibition Gardens, Lytton Street and Melbourne University.

measles that bite (in the night-time)

Image Credit: Barnett, F. Oswald. 1935. State Library of Victoria. [Carlton. Kitchen interior with woman and three children]
Image URL: https://find.slv.vic.gov.au/permalink/61SLV_INST/1sev8ar/alma9917771643607636
F. Oswald Barnett's Notes: —
Image Description: Interior view of kitchen with open fireplace. Containers and utensils sit on the mantelpiece above the fireplace. A woman and three children are seated around a wooden table in front of the fire.

a tumbledown alley (a mostly-dry home)

    Image Credit: *Barnett, F. Oswald. 1935. State Library of Victoria. [Carlton. Little Grattan Street, opposite Teachers' Training College]*
    Image URL: *https://find.slv.vic.gov.au/permalink/61SLV_INST/1sev8ar/alma9917774183607636*
    F. Oswald Barnett's Notes: *Carlton. Little Grattan Street opposite Teachers' Training College, University.*
    Image Description: *View across a narrow street with narrow footpaths to a group of single-storey weatherboard houses, one with a wooden picket fence. Double-storey brick houses stand behind. A high corrugated-iron fence appears in the right foreground.*

a shank's pony ride (from little barkly street)

    Image Credit: *Barnett, F. Oswald. 1935. State Library of Victoria. [Carlton. Little Barkly Street]*
    Image URL: *https://find.slv.vic.gov.au/permalink/61SLV_INST/1sev8ar/alma9917771713607636*
    F. Oswald Barnett's Notes: *Carlton. Little Barkly Street. This house is built onto the rear of an allotment facing Barkly Street.*
    Image Description: *View down a street bordered by narrow footpaths, brick walls and a house. Other houses are visible in the distance.*

everything (and our children)

    Image Credit: *Barnett, F. Oswald. 1935. State Library of Victoria. [Carlton. 99a Palmerston Street]*
    Image URL: *https://find.slv.vic.gov.au/permalink/61SLV_INST/1sev8ar/alma9917769593607636*
    F. Oswald Barnett's Notes: *Carlton. 99a Palmerston Street. House at end of lane. Stables in front.*
    Image Description: *View down a narrow bluestone-paved lane leading to a house. Two people stand on the verandah. A buggy is partially visible in front of the house.*

lucky children (with horses)

    Image Credit: *Barnett, F. Oswald. 1935. State Library of Victoria. [Carlton. Entrance to a slum pocket]*
    Image URL: *https://find.slv.vic.gov.au/permalink/61SLV_INST/1sev8ar/alma9917771903607636*
    F. Oswald Barnett's Notes: *Carlton. Entrance to a slum pocket known as Carlow Place. The pool in the foreground was drainage from a stable. Some words of the original caption were crossed out and amended by hand to read: "Entrance to a slum pocket in Carlton (City of Melbourne)."*
    Image Description: *Two children play in a pool of water in a bluestone-paved street. Houses stand in the background.*

sweet sounds (in the backyard)

Image Credit: Barnett, F. Oswald. 1935. State Library of Victoria. [Carlton. Plan showing house built on Barkly Street frontage and house at the rear facing Little Barkly Street]
Image URL: https://find.slv.vic.gov.au/permalink/61SLV_INST/1sev8ar/alma9917774003607636
F. Oswald Barnett's Notes: Carlton. Plan showing house built on Barkly Street frontage and house at the rear facing Little Barkly Street. See photograph No. 2. Notice the total depth of the land is 72 ft and frontage 13 ft. Under the Health Act each house should have at least 1650 sq. ft. of land. These two houses occupy a block of less than 1000 sq. ft.
Image Description: Hand-coloured annotated plan showing two adjoining houses and their yards.

shelter wood (from all storms)

Image Credit: Barnett, F. Oswald. 1935. State Library of Victoria. Carlton. Washhouse and bath-room, 48 Palmerston Street [picture].
Image URL: https://find.slv.vic.gov.au/permalink/61SLV_INST/1sev8ar/alma9917772013607636
F. Oswald Barnett's Notes: Carlton. Washhouse and bath-room, 48 Palmerston Street. The only water laid on is the tap over the gully trap. The only washing convenience the hand basin on the box. The piece of canvas was erected for the purpose of keeping the wood dry.
Image Description: Washing and bathing facilities in a backyard setting. Woman and girl standing near the clothes line.

hard for the weather (to find us)

Image Credit: Barnett, F. Oswald. 1935. State Library of Victoria. Carlton. Carlton Place [picture].
Image URL: https://find.slv.vic.gov.au/permalink/61SLV_INST/1sev8ar/alma9917772023607636
F. Oswald Barnett's Notes: Carlton. Carlton Place, Carlton. Four brick cottages built on to a right-of-way off a right-of-way at the rear of a factory.
Image Description: View of man in a suit and bowler hat, and a cat, standing on a grassy area beside a row of brick dwellings. Brick walls to the right and behind.

a little less cold (a little more mould)

Image Credit: Barnett, F. Oswald. 1935. State Library of Victoria. Carlton. Broken roof stuffed with old clothing [picture].
Image URL: https://find.slv.vic.gov.au/permalink/61SLV_INST/1sev8ar/alma9917774163607636
F. Oswald Barnett's Notes: —
Image Description: Close-up of a shingle or slate rooftop partially overlaid with garments. Chimney in the background.

getting by (at a shilling a foot)

Image Credit: *Barnett, F. Oswald. 1935. State Library of Victoria. Carlton. No. 48 Palmerston Street [picture].*
Image URL: *https://find.slv.vic.gov.au/permalink/61SLV_INST/1sev8ar/alma9917771513607636*
F. Oswald Barnett's Notes: *Carlton. No. 48 Palmerston Street, Carlton. Frontage 13'. Rent 11/6.*
Image Description: *Row of house façades with narrow frontages.*

a nine foot wingspan (would never fit)

Image Credit: *Barnett, F. Oswald. 1935. State Library of Victoria. Carlton. Ormond Place [picture].*
Image URL: *https://find.slv.vic.gov.au/permalink/61SLV_INST/1sev8ar/alma9917771533607636*
F. Oswald Barnett's Notes: *Carlton. Ormond Place, Carlton. 9' wide.*
Image Description: *View down a narrow bluestone-paved lane. Houses with front picket fences along the left side.*

a meal costs a penny (if your dad doesn't work)

Image Credit: *Barnett, F. Oswald. 1935. State Library of Victoria. Carlton. Group portrait of a man and children outside a church [picture].*
Image URL: *https://find.slv.vic.gov.au/permalink/61SLV_INST/1sev8ar/alma9917771923607636*
F. Oswald Barnett's Notes: *Carlton. The mid-day muster of children of unemployed parents, who are provided by the Presbyterian Church with a hot dinner for the price of one penny, the strict condition being: 'Father must be unemployed'.*
Image Description: *Man with a large group of children standing in, and in front of, the entrance to a church.*

that's all right (nobody looks)

Image Credit: *Barnett, F. Oswald. 1935. State Library of Victoria. Carlton. Lavatory, 48 Palmerston Street [picture].*
Image URL: *https://find.slv.vic.gov.au/permalink/61SLV_INST/1sev8ar/alma9917771493607636*
F. Oswald Barnett's Notes: *Lavatory, 48 Palmerston Street. Faces south. Door missing.*
Image Description: *Interior of brick lavatory building. No door.*

no one (nothing)

Image Credit: *Barnett, F. Oswald. 1935. State Library of Victoria. Carlton. Two mothers [picture].*
Image URL: *https://find.slv.vic.gov.au/permalink/61SLV_INST/1sev8ar/alma9917771763607636*
F. Oswald Barnett's Notes: *Carlton. Two mothers. Both were under the influence of liquor. The doctor with me said that one baby had been very ill and had recovered, but now would die owing to neglect.*
Image Description: *Two shabbily dressed women holding babies, standing in an open gateway.*

home (in the cobblestones)

>**Image Credit:** Barnett, F. Oswald. 1935. State Library of Victoria. Carlton. Somerset Place [picture].
>**Image URL:** https://find.slv.vic.gov.au/permalink/61SLV_INST/1sev8ar/alma9917771503607636
>**F. Oswald Barnett's Notes:** Carlton. Somerset Place. It is stated that there is at least one child in every house in this street who has had diphtheria. The conditions of the gutter as shown in the photo would tend to support this contention.
>**Image Description:** Street paved with bluestone, with houses on either side. Water in open gutters. Child standing in the street.

cricket and dogs and kids (and hopscotch)

>**Image Credit:** Barnett, F. Oswald. 1935. State Library of Victoria. Carlton. David Street [picture].
>**Image URL:** https://find.slv.vic.gov.au/permalink/61SLV_INST/1sev8ar/alma9917771873607636
>**F. Oswald Barnett's Notes:** Carlton. David Street. Noted for the number of children. Handwritten pencil inscription on verso: "David St, Carlton. 18' wide."
>**Image Description:** View down paved street. Two-storey brick houses on either side. Child leaning over front fence on left side. Two dogs, child, and other single-storey houses visible at end of street.

almost educated (not likely)

>**Image Credit:** Barnett, F. Oswald. 1935. State Library of Victoria. Carlton. Entrance to a slum pocket in Elgin Street [picture].
>**Image URL:** https://find.slv.vic.gov.au/permalink/61SLV_INST/1sev8ar/alma9917772043607636
>**F. Oswald Barnett's Notes:** Carlton. Entrance to a slum pocket in Elgin Street. Within a few yards of the University.
>**Image Description:** View across a wet street to a two-storey brick house with a large tree beside it. Partial views of single-storey houses and a parked car included.

no-one (to say boo)

>**Image Credit:** Barnett, F. Oswald. 1935. State Library of Victoria. Carlton. Entrance to Airdale Place [picture].
>**Image URL:** https://find.slv.vic.gov.au/permalink/61SLV_INST/1sev8ar/alma9917771943607636
>**F. Oswald Barnett's Notes:** Carlton. Entrance to Airdale Place through a right-of-way 9' wide, narrowing to a bottleneck 4'6" wide.
>**Image Description:** View down a narrow bluestone-paved lane to the Place beyond. No footpaths. Weatherboard building on right, brick building on left. Other buildings visible in background.

no complaints (the walls are thin)

> **Image Credit:** *Barnett, F. Oswald. 1935. State Library of Victoria. Carlton. Airedale Place [picture].*
> **Image URL:** *https://find.slv.vic.gov.au/permalink/61SLV_INST/1sev8ar/alma9917771843607636*
> **F. Oswald Barnett's Notes:** *Carlton. Airedale Place. Footpath 4' wide. Former front garden 6' wide. Faces rear of brick factory. Handwritten inscription in blue ink on verso: "Slums. Airedale Place, Carlton. 4 houses in a 4' lane off a street less than 20 ft wide."*
> **Image Description:** *View down narrow alley. Brick buildings on either side.*

slippy to the lavatory (in the winter)

> **Image Credit:** *Barnett, F. Oswald. 1935. State Library of Victoria. Carlton. Slum pocket [picture].*
> **Image URL:** *https://find.slv.vic.gov.au/permalink/61SLV_INST/1sev8ar/alma9917771673607636*
> **F. Oswald Barnett's Notes:** *Carlton (circa 1930) Slum pocket. Houses built on a depth of 13', including the front garden. No back yard; right-of-way doubles as drying ground. Props and clothes hung out to dry. Ramshackle shed contains lavatory, washhouse, and bath-room. Water is taken from tap over gully trap on far side of right-of-way.*
> **Image Description:** *View down bluestone lane. Brick houses with picket fences on left side. Two women visible in small front gardens.*

I live here (in collingwood)

> **Image Credit:** *Barnett, F. Oswald. 1935. State Library of Victoria. Collingwood from the Town Hall tower [picture].*
> **Image URL:** *https://find.slv.vic.gov.au/permalink/61SLV_INST/1sev8ar/alma9917770043607636*
> **F. Oswald Barnett's Notes:** *—*
> **Image Description:** *Aerial view of housing and factories.*

to keep out (of the night)

> **Image Credit:** *Barnett, F. Oswald. 1935. State Library of Victoria. Collingwood. Little Oxford Street [picture].*
> **Image URL:** *https://find.slv.vic.gov.au/permalink/61SLV_INST/1sev8ar/alma9917772373607636*
> **F. Oswald Barnett's Notes:** *Collingwood. Little Oxford Street. One-roomed house.*
> **Image Description:** *View of street with single-storey brick, weatherboard, and stone houses along right side. Girl standing on footpath outside one-roomed house. Two boys standing in middle of road; car parked on left side.*

little charles we hope for (and bread)

> **Image Credit:** *Barnett, F. Oswald. 1935. State Library of Victoria. Abbotsford. Little Charles Street [picture].*
> **Image URL:** *https://find.slv.vic.gov.au/permalink/61SLV_INST/1sev8ar/alma9917772283607636*
> **F. Oswald Barnett's Notes:** *Collingwood. Little Charles Street, Abbotsford. Twenty-three houses on one side of street; on the opposite side, back-yards, marine yards and stables.*
> **Image Description:** *View down narrow street. Weatherboard houses on right side, back yard fences on left.*

ooh look (the premier has come)

Image Credit: *Barnett, F. Oswald. 1935. State Library of Victoria. Collingwood. Premier enters 3 R house [picture].*
Image URL: *https://find.slv.vic.gov.au/permalink/61SLV_INST/1sev8ar/alma9917774393607636*
F. Oswald Barnett's Notes: *Collingwood. Premier enters three-roomed house occupied by two adults and eight children. Hand-printed inscription on verso: "Barnett 5th from left opening gate."*
Image Description: *View across street to a group of four men and a woman outside a small weatherboard house, first man about to open gate. Two other women nearby on footpath, one pushing a pram. Dog on footpath behind her. Partial view of car further down street outside brick building.*

an old bag (but it helps)

Image Credit: *Barnett, F. Oswald. 1935. State Library of Victoria. Collingwood. Weatherboard house and yard [picture].*
Image URL: *https://find.slv.vic.gov.au/permalink/61SLV_INST/1sev8ar/alma9917777253607636*
F. Oswald Barnett's Notes: *Collingwood. Same bag covering window for ten years.*
Image Description: *Close-up view of side of weatherboard house with one window covered with fabric. Yard in background.*

sunshine and fresh air (for the bedding)

Image Credit: *Barnett, F. Oswald. 1935. State Library of Victoria. Collingwood. Victoria Place [picture].*
Image URL: *https://find.slv.vic.gov.au/permalink/61SLV_INST/1sev8ar/alma9917772223607636*
F. Oswald Barnett's Notes: *Collingwood. Victoria Place. Back yard. Rain comes in so bedding is hung out to dry on fine days.*
Image Description: *View through verandah posts to back yard with bedding hung on clothes line and over metal frame. Corrugated iron fence in background.*

whichever way you look (it's a LOT of mouths)

Image Credit: *Barnett, F. Oswald. 1935. State Library of Victoria. Collingwood. No. 12 Hood Street [picture].*
Image URL: *https://find.slv.vic.gov.au/permalink/61SLV_INST/1sev8ar/alma9917772173607636*
F. Oswald Barnett's Notes: *Collingwood. No. 12 Hood Street. Man, wife and eight children. Three rooms. Sustenance house; rent 8/-. No bath.*
Image Description: *Group of children standing or sitting by picket fence in front of weatherboard house.*

in and out (like a ginger beer stopper)

Image Credit: *Barnett, F. Oswald. 1935. State Library of Victoria. Collingwood. Premier entering condemned house [picture].*
Image URL: *https://find.slv.vic.gov.au/permalink/61SLV_INST/1sev8ar/alma9917774273607636*
F. Oswald Barnett's Notes: *Barnett far right in group (in black hat and overcoat).*
Image Description: *Group of men in hats and overcoats at entrance to brick house. Dilapidated fence around house. Other men approaching in street outside.*

just shut up (and do)

Image Credit: *Barnett, F. Oswald. 1935. State Library of Victoria. Collingwood. Rear of No. 5 Hood Street [picture].*
Image URL: *https://find.slv.vic.gov.au/permalink/61SLV_INST/1sev8ar/alma9917772163607636*
F. Oswald Barnett's Notes: *Rear of No. 5 Hood Street, showing washhouse and bath-room. Kerosene tin as the copper. Only water laid on is over gully trap. Sustenance house; rent 9/- a week. Man, wife and six children.*
Image Description: *View of external washing and bathing facilities and clothes line at rear of house.*

very close (in glasgow street)

Image Credit: *Barnett, F. Oswald. 1935. State Library of Victoria. Collingwood. Corner Glasgow & Silver Streets [picture].*
Image URL: *https://find.slv.vic.gov.au/permalink/61SLV_INST/1sev8ar/alma9917772303607636*
F. Oswald Barnett's Notes: *Collingwood. Corner Glasgow and Silver Streets. Two houses.*
Image Description: *Corner view of single-storey weatherboard house with corrugated iron fence behind and two-storey brick house opposite. Timber stacked roof-high in yard behind weatherboard house.*

useless in the wet (and a trial through summer)

Image Credit: *Barnett, F. Oswald. 1935. State Library of Victoria. Collingwood. Back yard [picture].*
Image URL: *https://find.slv.vic.gov.au/permalink/61SLV_INST/1sev8ar/alma9917774333607636*
F. Oswald Barnett's Notes: *—*
Image Description: *View of back yard showing corner of house, gully trap with tap above, clothing hanging on line and weatherboard lavatory building.*

what we have to do (top-to-toe)

> **Image Credit:** Barnett, F. Oswald. 1935. State Library of Victoria. Collingwood. Plan of house, No. 12 Hood Street [picture].
> **Image URL:** https://find.slv.vic.gov.au/permalink/61SLV_INST/1sev8ar/alma9917774053607636
> **F. Oswald Barnett's Notes:** Collingwood. Plan of house No. 12 Hood Street, showing how two adults and eight children can live in three-roomed house.
> **Image Description:** Hand-coloured annotated plan of house with 12 ft frontage.

hell to hang (inside)

> **Image Credit:** Barnett, F. Oswald. 1935. State Library of Victoria. Collingwood. Open-air washhouse [picture].
> **Image URL:** https://find.slv.vic.gov.au/permalink/61SLV_INST/1sev8ar/alma9917774413607636
> **F. Oswald Barnett's Notes:** Collingwood. Open-air washhouse. Typical of thousands.
> **Image Description:** View of back yard with outdoor laundry facilities. Woman at copper washing clothes; two young children next to her. Garments hanging on clothes line. Gully trap, tap and partial view of back of house visible in background.

high and mighty (in hood street)

> **Image Credit:** Barnett, F. Oswald. 1935. State Library of Victoria. Collingwood. Premier entering condemned house [picture].
> **Image URL:** https://find.slv.vic.gov.au/permalink/61SLV_INST/1sev8ar/alma9917774273607636
> **F. Oswald Barnett's Notes:** Barnett far right in group (in black hat and overcoat).
> **Image Description:** Group of men in hats and overcoats at entrance to brick house. Dilapidated fence around house. Other men approaching in street outside.

not in a window (maybe in a bottle)

> **Image Credit:** Barnett, F. Oswald. 1935. State Library of Victoria. Collingwood. Glasshouse Street [picture].
> **Image URL:** https://find.slv.vic.gov.au/permalink/61SLV_INST/1sev8ar/alma9917772353607636
> **F. Oswald Barnett's Notes:** Collingwood. Glasshouse Street viewed from the other end.
> **Image Description:** View of road paved with bluestone disappearing between corrugated iron fence on left and paling fence on right. Weatherboard house behind paling fence. Large brick building bearing words "Foy & Gibson" visible in background.

more damage (as if)

Image Credit: *Barnett, F. Oswald. 1935. State Library of Victoria. Collingwood. Dilapidated verandah floor [picture].*
Image URL: *https://find.slv.vic.gov.au/permalink/61SLV_INST/1sev8ar/alma9917777333607636*
F. Oswald Barnett's Notes: *Collingwood. Showing decay in verandah floor.*
Image Description: *Close-up view of verandah floorboards in poor condition.*

hessian and paper (none at all)

Image Credit: *Barnett, F. Oswald. 1935. State Library of Victoria. Collingwood. Rokeby Street [picture].*
Image URL: *https://find.slv.vic.gov.au/permalink/61SLV_INST/1sev8ar/alma9917772273607636*
F. Oswald Barnett's Notes: *Collingwood. Rokeby Street. Abutting on this street and on the left are some of the worst streets in Collingwood: Northumberland Street, Glasgow Street, Waterloo Road, Glasshouse Road, Glasshouse Street. Partitions between houses made of hessian and paper.*
Image Description: *View down street with long row of adjoining houses on right. Some houses have picket fences. Woman and child visible on footpath.*

bail the bath (and seal the door)

Image Credit: *Barnett, F. Oswald. 1935. State Library of Victoria. Little Harmsworth Street, Collingwood [picture].*
Image URL: *https://find.slv.vic.gov.au/permalink/61SLV_INST/1sev8ar/alma9917772083607636*
F. Oswald Barnett's Notes: *Little Harmsworth Street, Collingwood. Three rooms, bath-room and small detached kitchen. Window in top left-hand corner lights bath-room. Bath drainage blocked; has to be baled out. One room badly bug-infested and uninhabitable. Handwritten inscription above photograph: "Little Harmsworth Street, Collingwood."*
Image Description: *View down street bordered mainly by back yard fences. No footpaths. Weatherboard house on right opens onto street. Person and other houses visible at end of street.*

the best we can (or eaten alive)

Image Credit: *Barnett, F. Oswald. 1935. State Library of Victoria. Collingwood. Plan of cottage, Little Harmsworth Street [picture].*
Image URL: *https://find.slv.vic.gov.au/permalink/61SLV_INST/1sev8ar/alma9917776193607636*
F. Oswald Barnett's Notes: *Collingwood. Plan of cottage. Little Harmsworth Street. Three rooms usable. Two adults, four children. Bug-infested.*
Image Description: *N/A*

packed in (a good proposition)

    Image Credit: *Barnett, F. Oswald. 1935. State Library of Victoria. Collingwood. First house in Glasshouse Street [picture].*
    Image URL: *https://find.slv.vic.gov.au/permalink/61SLV_INST/1sev8ar/alma9917772253607636*
    F. Oswald Barnett's Notes: *Collingwood. Single-storey at front, double-storey at rear. Three rooms in all. Rent 8/6 per week. House made of wood resembling packing cases.*
    Image Description: *Partial corner view of wooden house with corrugated iron roof.*

all the air (to breathe)

    Image Credit: *Barnett, F. Oswald. 1935. State Library of Victoria. Collingwood. Glasshouse Street [picture].*
    Image URL: *https://find.slv.vic.gov.au/permalink/61SLV_INST/1sev8ar/alma9917772343607636*
    F. Oswald Barnett's Notes: *Collingwood. Glasshouse Street. Four-roomed house. Two rooms 11' x 10', two rooms 11' x 9'. Man, wife and seven children.*
    Image Description: *Single-storey weatherboard house with corrugated iron roof behind paling fence. Woman and child partially visible in left foreground.*

not proud (but our best)

    Image Credit: *Barnett, F. Oswald. 1935. State Library of Victoria. Collingwood. Glasshouse Street [picture].*
    Image URL: *https://find.slv.vic.gov.au/permalink/61SLV_INST/1sev8ar/alma9917777283607636*
    F. Oswald Barnett's Notes: —
    Image Description: *View down street paved with bluestone. Houses (some weatherboard) on either side. Multi-storey brick building visible in background.*

or something better (but they don't mind)

    Image Credit: *Barnett, F. Oswald. 1935. State Library of Victoria. Collingwood. Waterloo Road [picture].*
    Image URL: *https://find.slv.vic.gov.au/permalink/61SLV_INST/1sev8ar/alma9917772323607636*
    F. Oswald Barnett's Notes: *Collingwood. Waterloo Road.*
    Image Description: *View down bluestone-paved road. High fence and large brick building on right. Houses and other brick buildings on left. People visible at end of road.*

no I repeat no (slums in fitzroy)

    Image Credit: *Barnett, F. Oswald. 1935. State Library of Victoria. Fitzroy Town Hall [picture].*
    Image URL: *https://find.slv.vic.gov.au/permalink/61SLV_INST/1sev8ar/alma9917772653607636*
    F. Oswald Barnett's Notes: *Fitzroy Town Hall. In reply to government request, Fitzroy replied it had no slums.*
    Image Description: *Corner view of town hall showing tower, pediments and colonnades. Car parked outside.*

the beating heart (a place of pride)

>**Image Credit:** Barnett, F. Oswald. 1935. State Library of Victoria. Fitzroy. View of Victoria Parade [picture].
>**Image URL:** https://find.slv.vic.gov.au/permalink/61SLV_INST/1sev8ar/alma9917772393607636
>**F. Oswald Barnett's Notes:** Fitzroy. View of Victoria Parade from Fire Brigade Tower.
>**Image Description:** Aerial view of wide boulevard — Victoria Parade — with large buildings and houses on either side. Trees and tram-line in centre, including two trams. Building in right foreground bears words "Victorian Eye & Ear Hospital."

alive and dead (outside their doors)

>**Image Credit:** Barnett, F. Oswald. 1935. State Library of Victoria. Fitzroy. Market Street [picture].
>**Image URL:** https://find.slv.vic.gov.au/permalink/61SLV_INST/1sev8ar/alma9917772513607636
>**F. Oswald Barnett's Notes:** Market Street opposite Fitzroy Town Hall. Caption on copy photograph reads: "Fitzroy. Market Street. Town Hall at end."
>**Image Description:** View looking down street to grand building at end. Brick housing on either side of street.

no complaints (and no one listening)

>**Image Credit:** Barnett, F. Oswald. 1935. State Library of Victoria. Fitzroy. An apartment house [picture].
>**Image URL:** https://find.slv.vic.gov.au/permalink/61SLV_INST/1sev8ar/alma9917773233607636
>**F. Oswald Barnett's Notes:** Fitzroy. An apartment house, seven rooms and three sleep outs, a total of ten living rooms. Occupied by six men, six women and twelve children, total twenty-four persons.
>**Image Description:** Front view of two-storey house with three windows and doorway opening directly onto footpath. Fire hydrant on footpath.

something chronic (the key's not out)

>**Image Credit:** Barnett, F. Oswald. 1935. State Library of Victoria. Fitzroy. The key of the front door of the apartment house [picture].
>**Image URL:** https://find.slv.vic.gov.au/permalink/61SLV_INST/1sev8ar/alma9917773403607636
>**F. Oswald Barnett's Notes:** Fitzroy. The key of the front door. Inside on wall is pasted a notice: "the last person in at night please see that the front door is locked properly and shut the door gently." Notes concern how the last person ascertains they are last, drawing key through hole. Described as an easy means of access to immorality.
>**Image Description:** Close-up of closed door and jamb. Yale lock in door with round hole beneath it; key on chain hanging through hole. Another conventional keyhole beneath the key.

there's no kitchens (if you're on the susso)

Image Credit: *Barnett, F. Oswald. 1935. State Library of Victoria. Fitzroy. Three-storey apartment house [picture].*
Image URL: *https://find.slv.vic.gov.au/permalink/61SLV_INST/1sev8ar/alma9917773213607636*
F. Oswald Barnett's Notes: *Fitzroy. Three-storey apartment house of nine rooms, each ~12' x 14'. Let in single rooms at 5/- per week, 2/6 per night. Gas stove on penny-in-slot system, but most cooking done in rooms; rooms without fireplace use kerosene tin for cooking.*
Image Description: *Front view of three-storey house with four windows plus attic window. Wooden picket fence in front.*

chicken wire (to feel safer in the night)

Image Credit: *Barnett, F. Oswald. 1935. State Library of Victoria. Fitzroy. Little Napier Street [picture].*
Image URL: *https://find.slv.vic.gov.au/permalink/61SLV_INST/1sev8ar/alma9917772743607636*
F. Oswald Barnett's Notes: *Fitzroy. Little Napier Street, once known as Vendetta Street. Shows how windows were barricaded during "the feud."*
Image Description: *Window set in brick wall, secured with wire/metal grill.*

push and push back (it was war in little napier)

Image Credit: *Barnett, F. Oswald. 1935. State Library of Victoria. North Melbourne. Off Avon Place [picture].*
Image URL: *https://find.slv.vic.gov.au/permalink/61SLV_INST/1sev8ar/alma9917773303607636*
F. Oswald Barnett's Notes: *Fitzroy. Little Napier Street, showing barbed wire entanglements during "the feud."*
Image Description: *Close-up of wooden picket fence in front of house. Barbed wire strung along top of fence.*

the very devil (that leaves you numbed)

Image Credit: *Barnett, F. Oswald. 1935. State Library of Victoria. Fitzroy. Little George Street [picture].*
Image URL: *https://find.slv.vic.gov.au/permalink/61SLV_INST/1sev8ar/alma9917772593607636*
F. Oswald Barnett's Notes: *Fitzroy. Little George Street. Woman in picture intoxicated by Fitzroy's famous "rot gut" wine. Caption: "Fitz. L. George St. Woman drunk with 'rot gut.'"*
Image Description: *View down bluestone street. High corrugated iron fence and single-storey houses on left. Woman in dark clothing in street; another person at fence further down.*

almost enough rotgut (and close-by to boot)

Image Credit: *Barnett, F. Oswald. 1935. State Library of Victoria. Plan of inner portion, Fitzroy [picture].*
Image URL: *https://find.slv.vic.gov.au/permalink/61SLV_INST/1sev8ar/alma9917778543607636*
F. Oswald Barnett's Notes: *—*
Image Description: *Map of Fitzroy portion bounded by Victoria Parade, Johnston Street, Nicholson Street, and Smith Street. Numbers of hotels, wine shops, licensed grocers and delicensed hotels/wine shops marked.*

god and the brotherhood and the rain (to watch over us)

Image Credit: Barnett, F. Oswald. 1935. State Library of Victoria. Fitzroy. View from the Brotherhood of St. Lawrence [picture].
Image URL: https://find.slv.vic.gov.au/permalink/61SLV_INST/1sev8ar/alma9917772823607636
F. Oswald Barnett's Notes: View from Brotherhood of St. Lawrence, showing rear of four pairs of cottages, one in process of disappearing. No bathrooms; tenants wash in the open.
Image Description: Elevated view of back yards of cottages; roofs, chimneys, and other buildings visible in background.

a place for the kiddies (to play)

Image Credit: Barnett, F. Oswald. 1935. State Library of Victoria. Fitzroy. The only official playground [picture].
Image URL: https://find.slv.vic.gov.au/permalink/61SLV_INST/1sev8ar/alma9917773323607636
F. Oswald Barnett's Notes: Fitzroy. The only official playground, opposite Town Hall, bounded on north by ramshackle cottages.
Image Description: View across road to sparsely equipped playground. Fences and backs of houses in background.

a place to play (if you know what I mean)

Image Credit: Barnett, F. Oswald. 1935. State Library of Victoria. Fitzroy. Little Napier Street [picture].
Image URL: https://find.slv.vic.gov.au/permalink/61SLV_INST/1sev8ar/alma9917773263607636
F. Oswald Barnett's Notes: Fitzroy. Little Napier Street. Rear of terrace in Young Street. Vacant allotment is only playground in area except small playground opposite Town Hall.
Image Description: View across vacant allotment to rear of two-storey brick terrace. High continuous fence backs onto allotment. Three figures visible at far end.

a place (in the fitzroy night)

Image Credit: Barnett, F. Oswald. 1935. State Library of Victoria. Fitzroy. Rear view of house [picture].
Image URL: https://find.slv.vic.gov.au/permalink/61SLV_INST/1sev8ar/alma9917772713607636
F. Oswald Barnett's Notes: Fitzroy. Rear view of house owned by Fitzroy councillor. Not occupied for rent, but unemployed men crawl through wall openings. Interior strewn with straw used as bed.
Image Description: Exterior partial view of dilapidated brick building. Corrugated iron partially covers door and window openings.

alone we die (in marion street)

Image Credit: *Barnett, F. Oswald. 1935. State Library of Victoria. Fitzroy. A terrace of four houses in Marion Street [picture].*
Image URL: *https://find.slv.vic.gov.au/permalink/61SLV_INST/1sev8ar/alma9917772803607636*
F. Oswald Barnett's Notes: *Fitzroy. Terrace of four houses in Marion Street, each frontage ~8'. In first house, a woman lay dying with cancer; furniture consisted of a single bed, a chair, and small wash-hand stand. Room so small only one visitor at a time could be accommodated.*
Image Description: *Front view of terrace of four, single-storey houses. Two complete facades, each with one window and door. Two partial facades.*

it'll do (until something better)

Image Credit: *Barnett, F. Oswald. 1935. State Library of Victoria. Fitzroy. Fitzroy Street [picture].*
Image URL: *https://find.slv.vic.gov.au/permalink/61SLV_INST/1sev8ar/alma9917773333607636*
F. Oswald Barnett's Notes: *Fitzroy Street. House with attic room, 4 rooms. Land 17'6" x 94' (5 m x 28 m).*
Image Description: *Front view of brick house showing one window, a door, and attic window. Wooden picket fence in front.*

ten to her the rest to me (and the metho)

Image Credit: *Barnett, F. Oswald. 1935. State Library of Victoria. Fitzroy. The Bungalows [picture].*
Image URL: *https://find.slv.vic.gov.au/permalink/61SLV_INST/1sev8ar/alma9917772543607636*
F. Oswald Barnett's Notes: *Fitzroy. The Bungalows, Marion Street, rear of two-storey dwelling. Let to "methos" (methylated spirit drinkers) at 5/- per week. Landlady collects 10/- from pension each fortnight.*
Image Description: *View across bluestone-paved road to corrugated iron walls.*

tin is cold (so we do what we must)

Image Credit: *Barnett, F. Oswald. 1935. State Library of Victoria. Fitzroy. Tin house, Ward's Lane [picture].*
Image URL: *https://find.slv.vic.gov.au/permalink/61SLV_INST/1sev8ar/alma9917772673607636*
F. Oswald Barnett's Notes: *Fitzroy. Tin house, Ward's Lane. Occupied by woman reputed to be a receiver of stolen goods.*
Image Description: *View down bluestone-paved lane. Paling fence on right, single-storey brick houses on left; one with tin structure attached. Double-storey houses in background.*

three by three no bathroom (in argyle street)

Image Credit: Barnett, F. Oswald. 1935. State Library of Victoria. Fitzroy. Argyle Street [picture].
Image URL: https://find.slv.vic.gov.au/permalink/61SLV_INST/1sev8ar/alma9917772843607636
F. Oswald Barnett's Notes: Fitzroy. Argyle Street. Frontage 9′ x 35′. Each house contains three rooms, 9′ x 9′, no bathrooms. Rent 10/6 per week.
Image Description: View across street to terrace of three brick houses with corrugated iron roofs. Man standing outside first house. Multi-storey brick building with external stairway visible in background.

it's all right (if you can't see the damp)

Image Credit: Barnett, F. Oswald. 1935. State Library of Victoria. Napier Street, Fitzroy, east side opposite Town Hall [picture].
Image URL: https://find.slv.vic.gov.au/permalink/61SLV_INST/1sev8ar/alma9917773373607636
F. Oswald Barnett's Notes: Fitzroy. Young Street [actually Napier Street], houses opposite Town Hall. Creche and kindergarten in centre. Two-storey houses with inner rooms lacking direct light or ventilation; very damp, walls stained; lath tacked across ceiling corner to prevent collapse.
Image Description: View across road to row of two-storey brick terrace houses opening onto footpath. People visible on footpath/doorsteps; car parked; two men pushing cart in distance.

the sun shines somewhere (not here)

Image Credit: Barnett, F. Oswald. 1935. State Library of Victoria. [North Melbourne] Erskine Place [picture].
Image URL: https://find.slv.vic.gov.au/permalink/61SLV_INST/1sev8ar/alma9917774513607636
F. Oswald Barnett's Notes: N. Melb. Erskine Place. Four pairs, two-storey dwellings; maximum sun to bedroom 10 minutes daily.
Image Description: View down narrow curving street. Large two-storey brick buildings on left; lower brick walls on right. Children visible halfway down street.

hardwicke street (tenements up into the sky)

Image Credit: Barnett, F. Oswald. 1935. State Library of Victoria. North Melbourne. Hardwicke Street [picture].
Image URL: https://find.slv.vic.gov.au/permalink/61SLV_INST/1sev8ar/alma9917773553607636
F. Oswald Barnett's Notes: North Melbourne. Hardwicke Street. Dilapidated houses, rusty roofs. City Council proposed rebuilding: first scheme cottages (~£1375 each) abandoned; new scheme under discussion is tenement buildings.
Image Description: View down narrow bluestone-paved street. Narrow footpath; small single-storey houses on either side. Car parked halfway down on left.

accordion (enough)

Image Credit: Barnett, F. Oswald. 1935. State Library of Victoria. North Melbourne. No. 19 Byron Street [picture].
Image URL: https://find.slv.vic.gov.au/permalink/61SLV_INST/1sev8ar/alma9917773713607636
F. Oswald Barnett's Notes: North Melbourne. No. 19 Byron Street. Made entirely of corrugated iron.
Image Description: Front view of single-storey corrugated iron house with tall brick chimney. Wooden picket fence in front. Man in suit on footpath. Large brick building in background.

rats (that come a-calling)

Image Credit: Barnett, F. Oswald. 1935. State Library of Victoria. [North Melbourne] Premier leaving rat-infested cottage [picture].
Image URL: https://find.slv.vic.gov.au/permalink/61SLV_INST/1sev8ar/alma9917774493607636
F. Oswald Barnett's Notes: N. Melb. Premier leaving rat-infested cottage. Inscription on verso: Barnett 4th from left in black bowler hat.
Image Description: Man emerging from weatherboard house. Group of six men standing outside, all in overcoats and hats.

just like that (bastard)

Image Credit: Barnett, F. Oswald. 1935. State Library of Victoria. [House, North Melbourne] [picture].
Image URL: https://find.slv.vic.gov.au/permalink/61SLV_INST/1sev8ar/alma9917774453607636
F. Oswald Barnett's Notes: North Melbourne. House from which mother and son were evicted.
Image Description: Front view of single-storey weatherboard house with door on left and window on right; window covered with corrugated iron. Picket fence and gate in front.

ah well (the trough's under cover)

Image Credit: Barnett, F. Oswald. 1935. State Library of Victoria. North Melbourne. Washhouse, Erskine Place [picture].
Image URL: https://find.slv.vic.gov.au/permalink/61SLV_INST/1sev8ar/alma9917773623607636
F. Oswald Barnett's Notes: North Melbourne. Washhouse, Erskine Place. Weatherboards missing on both North and East sides. Dole wood in right-hand corner. Note rubbish on roof.
Image Description: View across firewood through missing wall to interior laundry. Wash trough visible on right; clothing draped on left.

there are worse (we survive)

> **Image Credit:** Barnett, F. Oswald. 1935. State Library of Victoria. North Melbourne. No. 19 Byron Street [picture].
> **Image URL:** https://find.slv.vic.gov.au/permalink/61SLV_INST/1sev8ar/alma9917773693607636
> **F. Oswald Barnett's Notes:** North Melbourne. Close-up view of roof of house No. 19 Byron Street.
> **Image Description:** Partial close-up of dilapidated corrugated iron roof. Part of brick chimney visible behind.

quiet sunshine (ten minutes a day)

> **Image Credit:** Barnett, F. Oswald. 1935. State Library of Victoria. North Melbourne. Erskine Place [picture].
> **Image URL:** https://find.slv.vic.gov.au/permalink/61SLV_INST/1sev8ar/alma9917773703607636
> **F. Oswald Barnett's Notes:** North Melbourne. Erskine Place. Right-of-way off a right-of-way. Four pairs of two-storey brick cottages, four rooms each (two downstairs, two upstairs). No windows on floor facing right-of-way; light enters front room only ~10 minutes per day.
> **Image Description:** View down narrow bluestone-paved lane, bordered by large brick building on left and brick walls on right. Two wooden doors open into lane on left.

damp enough (to make you sick)

> **Image Credit:** Barnett, F. Oswald. 1935. State Library of Victoria. [North Melbourne. Living room interior] [picture].
> **Image URL:** https://find.slv.vic.gov.au/permalink/61SLV_INST/1sev8ar/alma9917777363607636
> **F. Oswald Barnett's Notes:** North Melbourne. Showing damp wall in living room.
> **Image Description:** Corner of room showing stained wall and ceiling. Broom leaning against wall. Partial view of glass-fronted cupboard with crockery inside.

it means nothing (when it has always been)

> **Image Credit:** Barnett, F. Oswald. 1935. State Library of Victoria. North Melbourne. Two two-storied houses [picture].
> **Image URL:** https://find.slv.vic.gov.au/permalink/61SLV_INST/1sev8ar/alma9917773663607636
> **F. Oswald Barnett's Notes:** North Melbourne. Two two-storey houses, frontage 9' on right-of-way. Front door also functions as window. Drain in bottom left corner carries drainage from back-yards underneath house.
> **Image Description:** Close-up front view of two houses, each with small verandah, steps, and wooden paling fence. Corrugated iron fence partially visible left foreground.

to the copper (all the money went)

Image Credit: *Barnett, F. Oswald. 1935. State Library of Victoria. North Melbourne. Copper in Erskine Place [picture].*
Image URL: *https://find.slv.vic.gov.au/permalink/61SLV_INST/1sev8ar/alma9917773553607636*
F. Oswald Barnett's Notes: *Landlord refused to mend copper unless tenant paid extra 6d./week (from 10/- to 10/6). Tenant initially withheld two weeks' rent; landlord threatened eviction; tenant paid up. Copper since mended.*
Image Description: *Dilapidated laundry interior. Copper set in broken brickwork; trough to right. Single taps above copper/trough; large tin container underneath.*

the rat goes on (forever)

Image Credit: *Barnett, F. Oswald. 1935. State Library of Victoria. [Kitchen interior, North Melbourne] [picture].*
Image URL: *https://find.slv.vic.gov.au/permalink/61SLV_INST/1sev8ar/alma9917774463607636*
F. Oswald Barnett's Notes: *North Melbourne. Broken hearth and rat hole in floor.*
Image Description: *Partial room view showing dilapidated wood-burning stove on left; flat iron and kettle on top. Firewood on floor in front. Straw broom in corner; wire bed frame propped up on right.*

it's no good (half asleep)

Image Credit: *Barnett, F. Oswald. 1935. State Library of Victoria. [External bathing facilities, North Melbourne] [picture].*
Image URL: *https://find.slv.vic.gov.au/permalink/61SLV_INST/1sev8ar/alma9917774423607636*
F. Oswald Barnett's Notes: *North Melbourne. Only bathroom, used on cold/frosty morning.*
Image Description: *Backyard bathing facilities. Fully clothed man washing face over large tin basin; tap above with running water; partial view of mirror on wall/fence.*

we will survive (baby mine)

Image Credit: *Barnett, F. Oswald. 1935. State Library of Victoria. North Melbourne. Canning Place [picture].*
Image URL: *https://find.slv.vic.gov.au/permalink/61SLV_INST/1sev8ar/alma9917773463607636*
F. Oswald Barnett's Notes: *North Melbourne. Canning Place, lane off lane; houses face backyards. Newest houses; near-end houses have no front windows. Most have gardens. Woman in first house saved maternity bonus; last baby born without anaesthetic/doctor.*
Image Description: *View down bluestone-paved lane with high fences left, weatherboard houses with lower fences right. Other houses visible at lane end; bicycle leaning against fence.*

tin (not gingerbread)

Image Credit: *Barnett, F. Oswald. 1935. State Library of Victoria. North Melbourne. No. 19 Byron Street [picture].*
Image URL: *https://find.slv.vic.gov.au/permalink/61SLV_INST/1sev8ar/alma9917777403607636*
F. Oswald Barnett's Notes: *–*
Image Description: *Man in suit standing in front of corrugated iron house. Wooden picket fence between man and house.*

no room so (that's fair)

Image Credit: *Barnett, F. Oswald. 1935. State Library of Victoria. North Melbourne. Group of children in Erskine Place [picture].*
Image URL: *https://find.slv.vic.gov.au/permalink/61SLV_INST/1sev8ar/alma9917773673607636*
F. Oswald Barnett's Notes: *North Melbourne. Group of children in Erskine Place.*
Image Description: *View down narrow bluestone-paved lane. Group of eight children standing in lane. Lane bordered by large brick building left and brick walls right.*

there are some (with gutter)

Image Credit: *Barnett, F. Oswald. 1935. State Library of Victoria. North Melbourne. Avon Place [picture].*
Image URL: *https://find.slv.vic.gov.au/permalink/61SLV_INST/1sev8ar/alma9917773483607636*
F. Oswald Barnett's Notes: *North Melbourne. Avon Place. Another 9' right-of-way. Houses on both sides.*
Image Description: *View down narrow bluestone-paved street. Brick and weatherboard houses, some double storey, on either side. Dilapidated wood paling fence in right foreground. Single storey house visible at end of lane.*

mind your own (and draw the awning down)

Image Credit: *Barnett, F. Oswald. 1935. State Library of Victoria. North Melbourne. Off Avon Pl. [picture].*
Image URL: *https://find.slv.vic.gov.au/permalink/61SLV_INST/1sev8ar/alma9917777423607636*
F. Oswald Barnett's Notes: *North Melbourne. Off Avon Place. Note electric light.*
Image Description: *Close-up front view of weatherboard house with verandah enclosed by wooden picket fence.*

bad dreams (are dreamt in twilight)

Image Credit: *Barnett, F. Oswald. 1935. State Library of Victoria. [North Melbourne cottage] [picture].*
Image URL: *https://find.slv.vic.gov.au/permalink/61SLV_INST/1sev8ar/alma9917774443607636*
F. Oswald Barnett's Notes: *North Melbourne. A windowless cottage with 2 bedrooms above.*
Image Description: *Two-storey building. Central doorway on lower storey; steps leading up to right. Central window on upper storey. Small dog in yard in front of doorway.*

higgle and piggle (in north melbourne)

    Image Credit: *Barnett, F. Oswald. 1935. State Library of Victoria. North Melbourne. Row of four houses [picture].*
    Image URL: *https://find.slv.vic.gov.au/permalink/61SLV_INST/1sev8ar/alma9917773583607636*
    F. Oswald Barnett's Notes: *North Melbourne. Row of four houses onto right-of-way; fifth house around corner on right.*
    Image Description: *Terrace of single-storey brick houses. Dilapidated wooden picket fence between second and third houses.*

a house (yes it is)

    Image Credit: *Barnett, F. Oswald. 1935. State Library of Victoria. [Narrow walkway, Port Melbourne] [picture].*
    Image URL: *https://find.slv.vic.gov.au/permalink/61SLV_INST/1sev8ar/alma9917777443607636*
    F. Oswald Barnett's Notes: *Port Melbourne. House at rear 15/- p.w.*
    Image Description: *View down narrow walkway between high fence on left and weatherboard building on right. Other structures partially visible in background.*

not on your shoes (or legs)

    Image Credit: *Barnett, F. Oswald. 1935. State Library of Victoria. Port Melbourne. Church St. [picture].*
    Image URL: *https://find.slv.vic.gov.au/permalink/61SLV_INST/1sev8ar/alma9917775443607636*
    F. Oswald Barnett's Notes: *Church St. facing wall of Methodist church.*
    Image Description: *View down narrow bluestone-paved lane. Row of small houses left; brick wall of large building on right. Small house visible at end of lane. Corrugated iron fence in left foreground. Two people in lane.*

washing day (kids out clothes in)

    Image Credit: *Barnett, F. Oswald. 1935. State Library of Victoria. South Melbourne. Convery Sq. [picture].*
    Image URL: *https://find.slv.vic.gov.au/permalink/61SLV_INST/1sev8ar/alma9917775573607636*
    F. Oswald Barnett's Notes: *South Melbourne. Convery Square. Washing day; tub used as copper.*
    Image Description: *Exterior clothes washing facilities. Large tin tub on open fireplace. Fabric draped over side; garments hanging above left and right. Corrugated iron fence in background; firewood left of tub; packing case right.*

where else (right there)

    Image Credit: *Barnett, F. Oswald. 1935. State Library of Victoria. South Melbourne. Rear of houses facing York St. from Convery Sq. [picture].*
    Image URL: *https://find.slv.vic.gov.au/permalink/61SLV_INST/1sev8ar/alma9917777543607636*
    F. Oswald Barnett's Notes: *–*
    Image Description: *Backs of two-storey houses in dilapidated condition.*

more or less (it is whole)

    Image Credit: *Barnett, F. Oswald. 1935. State Library of Victoria. South Melbourne. Montague Pl. off Dorcas St. [picture].*
    Image URL: *https://find.slv.vic.gov.au/permalink/61SLV_INST/1sev8ar/alma9917777503607636*
    F. Oswald Barnett's Notes: *–*
    Image Description: *Weatherboard house left, partially obscured by high fence. Cart on road outside house.*

still like convicts (more or less)

    Image Credit: *Barnett, F. Oswald. 1935. State Library of Victoria. South Melbourne. Convery Sq. [picture].*
    Image URL: *https://find.slv.vic.gov.au/permalink/61SLV_INST/1sev8ar/alma9917777533607636*
    F. Oswald Barnett's Notes: *South Melbourne. Convery Square.*
    Image Description: *View across wasteland to corrugated iron house on right and another building behind. High fence along left side.*

singing (like you're dying)

    Image Credit: *Barnett, F. Oswald. 1935. State Library of Victoria. South Melbourne. House in Tin Pot Alley [picture].*
    Image URL: *https://find.slv.vic.gov.au/permalink/61SLV_INST/1sev8ar/alma9917775633607636*
    F. Oswald Barnett's Notes: *South Melbourne. House in Tin Pot Alley. Three rooms plus attic of iron; 80 years old.*
    Image Description: *Front and side view of corrugated iron house. Wooden gate and corrugated iron fence on right. Partial view of similar house left. Attic window visible.*

up and down (a little love goes)

    Image Credit: *Barnett, F. Oswald. 1935. State Library of Victoria. [Three children with dolls] [picture].*
    Image URL: *https://find.slv.vic.gov.au/permalink/61SLV_INST/1sev8ar/alma9917776153607636*
    F. Oswald Barnett's Notes: *–*
    Image Description: *House interior; close-up of three young children holding dolls, partially covered by bedclothes.*

a straitened alley (a straitened supper)

    Image Credit: *Barnett, F. Oswald. 1935. State Library of Victoria. [Melbourne. Street scene with terrace houses] [picture].*
    Image URL: *https://find.slv.vic.gov.au/permalink/61SLV_INST/1sev8ar/alma9917778173607636*
    F. Oswald Barnett's Notes: *–*
    Image Description: *View down narrow street showing small terrace houses with iron lace and front fences on right side, large brick buildings on left. Two figures visible on road in background.*

a whistle (through the hessian)

    Image Credit: *Barnett, F. Oswald. 1935. State Library of Victoria. Mildura. Bag hut [picture].*
    Image URL: *https://find.slv.vic.gov.au/permalink/61SLV_INST/1sev8ar/alma9917778633607636*
    F. Oswald Barnett's Notes: *Mildura. Bag hut, iron roof. Inhabited by widow and 4 children.*
    Image Description: *Dwelling with corrugated iron roof, surrounded by trees.*

bloody eyesore (to live in)

    Image Credit: *Barnett, F. Oswald. 1935. State Library of Victoria. [Street scene showing demolished building and back of two-storey house next door] [picture].*
    Image URL: *https://find.slv.vic.gov.au/permalink/61SLV_INST/1sev8ar/alma9917776043607636*
    F. Oswald Barnett's Notes: *–*
    Image Description: *Small brick structure and wooden posts amidst debris in foreground; other houses visible in background.*

pretty (the sty)

    Image Credit: *Barnett, F. Oswald. 1935. State Library of Victoria. [Melbourne. Wallpaper in damp house] [picture].*
    Image URL: *https://find.slv.vic.gov.au/permalink/61SLV_INST/1sev8ar/alma9917778073607636*
    F. Oswald Barnett's Notes: *Wallpaper in damp house (splendid hiding place for bugs).*
    Image Description: *Close-up of man pulling wallpaper aside to reveal wall underneath.*

a lullaby (of no harm tonight)

    Image Credit: *Barnett, F. Oswald. 1935. State Library of Victoria. [Interior, children's bedroom] [picture].*
    Image URL: *https://find.slv.vic.gov.au/permalink/61SLV_INST/1sev8ar/alma9917773983607636*
    F. Oswald Barnett's Notes: *–*
    Image Description: *Interior showing partial view of three children in separate beds, one a baby in bassinet. Patterned floor covering. Patterned wallpaper with cracks and stains.*

but (we couldn't anyway)

    Image Credit: *Barnett, F. Oswald. 1935. State Library of Victoria. [Woman and eight children at table] [picture].*
    Image URL: *https://find.slv.vic.gov.au/permalink/61SLV_INST/1sev8ar/alma9917775753607636*
    F. Oswald Barnett's Notes: *–*
    Image Description: *Children seated or standing around table, some eating bread. Woman cutting bread at left. Child in background reaching for object on wall.*

shabby (is the gift)

Image Credit: Barnett, F. Oswald. 1935. State Library of Victoria. [Father Christmas outside house handing out gifts] [picture].
Image URL: https://find.slv.vic.gov.au/permalink/61SLV_INST/1sev8ar/alma9917775693607636
F. Oswald Barnett's Notes: –
Image Description: Father Christmas outside weatherboard house handing gifts to children. Woman holding baby on doorstep.

from where they live (they're all vermin)

Image Credit: Barnett, F. Oswald. 1935. State Library of Victoria. [Exterior view of dilapidated houses] [picture].
Image URL: https://find.slv.vic.gov.au/permalink/61SLV_INST/1sev8ar/alma9917775953607636
F. Oswald Barnett's Notes: –
Image Description: View across open space to backs of houses. Person walking left. Other houses in background.

worth something (a little)

Image Credit: Barnett, F. Oswald. 1935. State Library of Victoria. [Laundry interior] [picture].
Image URL: https://find.slv.vic.gov.au/permalink/61SLV_INST/1sev8ar/alma9917775883607636
F. Oswald Barnett's Notes: –
Image Description: Brick laundry interior with two stone troughs right, copper far right, long narrow bench left. Windows in right and back walls.

ho ho ho (for little children)

Image Credit: Barnett, F. Oswald. 1935. State Library of Victoria. [Father Christmas in street with children] [picture].
Image URL: https://find.slv.vic.gov.au/permalink/61SLV_INST/1sev8ar/alma9917775673607636
F. Oswald Barnett's Notes: –
Image Description: Father Christmas and group of children walking down street. Brick house with wooden picket fence in background; other buildings visible.

we can be clean (at least)

Image Credit: Barnett, F. Oswald. 1935. State Library of Victoria. [Melbourne. Laundry interior] [picture].
Image URL: https://find.slv.vic.gov.au/permalink/61SLV_INST/1sev8ar/alma9917778083607636
F. Oswald Barnett's Notes: –
Image Description: Close-up of laundry interior; trough, hanging garments, firewood.

the hole is an odour (I'll have to fix myself)

   Image Credit: *Barnett, F. Oswald. 1935. State Library of Victoria. [Handwritten letter to Mr Barnett] [picture].*
   Image URL: *https://find.slv.vic.gov.au/permalink/61SLV_INST/1sev8ar/alma9917776213607636*
   F. Oswald Barnett's Notes: *–*
   Image Description: *– Handwritten letter addressed to Mr Barnett, dated 5 March 1935, from a person who had attended his lecture and slide presentation on the slum area.*

a hot bath (feed the heater)

   Image Credit: *Barnett, F. Oswald. 1935. State Library of Victoria. [Bathroom interior] [picture].*
   Image URL: *https://find.slv.vic.gov.au/permalink/61SLV_INST/1sev8ar/alma9917775853607636*
   F. Oswald Barnett's Notes: *–*
   Image Description: *Bathroom interior; partial view of bath with water heater right. Toilet left. Basin with single tap and window above, centre.*

a good man (look at the camera)

   Image Credit: *Barnett, F. Oswald. 1935. State Library of Victoria. [Man and boy standing in backyard] [picture].*
   Image URL: *https://find.slv.vic.gov.au/permalink/61SLV_INST/1sev8ar/alma9917776103607636*
   F. Oswald Barnett's Notes: *–*
   Image Description: *Man against wood paling fence left; boy leaning against wall right; gully trap with tap, copper, and table between them. Laundry under corrugated iron roof.*

right at the door (marvelous)

   Image Credit: *Barnett, F. Oswald. 1935. State Library of Victoria. [Melbourne. Terrace houses in narrow street] [picture].*
   Image URL: *https://find.slv.vic.gov.au/permalink/61SLV_INST/1sev8ar/alma9917778343607636*
   F. Oswald Barnett's Notes: *–*
   Image Description: *Narrow bluestone street. Terrace houses right (some weatherboard with iron lace). Factories left. Motorcycle with sidecar in street. Bicycle against fence.*

love your neighbour (keep no secrets)

   Image Credit: *Barnett, F. Oswald. 1935. State Library of Victoria. [Three men and a woman in narrow lane] [picture].*
   Image URL: *https://find.slv.vic.gov.au/permalink/61SLV_INST/1sev8ar/alma9917775903607636*
   F. Oswald Barnett's Notes: *Barnett on right.*
   Image Description: *Narrow bluestone lane bordered by brick building left, weatherboard right. Two men in suits and hats foreground, one near each building. Another man and woman in background.*

waste not (on temporary measures)

> **Image Credit:** *Barnett, F. Oswald. 1935. State Library of Victoria. [Two boys in shorts, coats, peaked caps, barefoot] [picture].*
> **Image URL:** *https://find.slv.vic.gov.au/permalink/61SLV_INST/1sev8ar/alma9917776123607636*
> **F. Oswald Barnett's Notes:** *–*
> **Image Description:** *No summary.*

not quite (like the parliament)

> **Image Credit:** *Barnett, F. Oswald. 1935. State Library of Victoria. Robertson inspects slum bathroom [picture].*
> **Image URL:** *https://find.slv.vic.gov.au/permalink/61SLV_INST/1sev8ar/alma9917777563607636*
> **F. Oswald Barnett's Notes:** *–*
> **Image Description:** *Group of men in coats and hats near exterior wall. One inspects bathing facilities: single upright tap and tin basin.*

life in a doll house (of some sort anyway)

> **Image Credit:** *Barnett, F. Oswald. 1935. State Library of Victoria. [Melbourne. Weatherboard house and brick building] [picture].*
> **Image URL:** *https://find.slv.vic.gov.au/permalink/61SLV_INST/1sev8ar/alma9917778193607636*
> **F. Oswald Barnett's Notes:** *–*
> **Image Description:** *Small weatherboard house with wooden fence and lacework abutting large brick building. Small pram in front.*

my bible and god (first)

> **Image Credit:** *Barnett, F. Oswald. 1935. State Library of Victoria. [Living room interior, woman at table] [picture].*
> **Image URL:** *https://find.slv.vic.gov.au/permalink/61SLV_INST/1sev8ar/alma9917776163607636*
> **F. Oswald Barnett's Notes:** *–*
> **Image Description:** *Walls adorned with photographs, pictures, and text.*

company (at meal times)

> **Image Credit:** *Barnett, F. Oswald. 1935. State Library of Victoria. [Single-storey terrace with women and children in front] [picture].*
> **Image URL:** *https://find.slv.vic.gov.au/permalink/61SLV_INST/1sev8ar/alma9917775943607636*
> **F. Oswald Barnett's Notes:** *–*
> **Image Description:** *Bluestone street view to long terrace. Wooden picket fences. Group of children and woman with baby on footpath. Pram in background; other people visible behind fences.*

no trouble (do they

>**Image Credit:** Barnett, F. Oswald. 1935. State Library of Victoria. [Melbourne housing] [picture].
>**Image URL:** https://find.slv.vic.gov.au/permalink/61SLV_INST/1sev8ar/alma9917778373607636
>**F. Oswald Barnett's Notes:** –
>**Image Description:** Bluestone street view; brick house right with child in doorway. Paling fence and foliage right foreground. Backs of houses, chimneys, corrugated iron sheets at street end. Large multi-storey brick building background.

no harm (walk to school)

>**Image Credit:** Barnett, F. Oswald. 1935. State Library of Victoria. [Melbourne. Weatherboard house] [picture].
>**Image URL:** https://find.slv.vic.gov.au/permalink/61SLV_INST/1sev8ar/alma9917778503607636
>**F. Oswald Barnett's Notes:** –
>**Image Description:** Narrow lane paved with bluestone; side view of weatherboard house. Small child leaning against front fence. Opposite building and fences visible. House and multi-storey building background.

whatever and wherever (a tin house)

>**Image Credit:** Barnett, F. Oswald. 1935. State Library of Victoria. Shepparton. Group of huts [picture].
>**Image URL:** https://find.slv.vic.gov.au/permalink/61SLV_INST/1sev8ar/alma9917778693607636
>**F. Oswald Barnett's Notes:** Shepparton.
>**Image Description:** Open space with wood pieces foreground. Group of huts of tin and fabric. Bicycle against tin hut right.

surprisingly good (for a sieve)

>**Image Credit:** Barnett, F. Oswald. 1935. State Library of Victoria. Mildura. Bag humpie [i.e. humpy] [picture].
>**Image URL:** https://find.slv.vic.gov.au/permalink/61SLV_INST/1sev8ar/alma9917778583607636
>**F. Oswald Barnett's Notes:** Mildura. Bag humpie. 2 adults, 2 children.
>**Image Description:** Open space view with two children near trees. Dwelling (perhaps hessian) left background. Fence and other construction right background.

quite cosy (really)

>**Image Credit:** Barnett, F. Oswald. 1935. State Library of Victoria. [Kitchen interior] [picture].
>**Image URL:** https://find.slv.vic.gov.au/permalink/61SLV_INST/1sev8ar/alma9917775833607636
>**F. Oswald Barnett's Notes:** –
>**Image Description:** Kitchen interior; gas burner with saucepan, stove in open fireplace. Chairs in front of stove. Containers on mantelpiece. Utensils on and hanging from shelving next to fireplace. Pictures on wall above mantelpiece.

What Readers Say

Small Town Kid

A modern-day minstrel. Highly recommended.
—A. F. (Australia)

Small Town Kid is a wonderful collection.
—S. T. (Australia)

Devil In The Wind

Trust me, this book will stay with you. Bravo!
—K. K. (USA)

Moving, beautiful, and terrible. I was left with a profound sense of respect, as well as a reminder that we should never take for granted every precious every moment of life.
—J. S. (South Africa)

The New Asylum

Words can't do justice to the emotional journey I travelled in (reading this collection).
—C. D. (Australia)

If I had to pick one book over the past year that has truly resonated with me, this would be it.
—K. B. (USA)

Walk Away Silver Heart

Instantly grips you by the throat in his step-by-step story of survival. Bravo!
—K. K. (USA)

Outstanding!
—B. T. (Australia)

A Kiss For The Worthy

A Celebration of Life Written in Thoughtful Bursts of Poetic Expression
—C M C (United States)

With every verse, I found myself reflecting about myself, my life, and the world.
—K

Rescue and Redemption

The passion of love in its many forms explored by one for another.
—J L (United States)

I've enjoyed every word, every breath. Every moment within the life of these stories.
—C D (Australia)

Sheep On The Somme

Museums and archivists take note--sell this in your gift shops, preserve it in your archives. Professors, teachers--share with your students.
—A R C (United States)

(This) book is a beautiful and graphic tribute to all those brave men and women who gave their lives for their countries between 1914 and 1918.
—R C (South Africa)

Ida: Searching for The Jazz Baby

I found myself deeply moved by the presentation of Ida's elusive, illusionary life.
—E G (United States)

He gives her a depth and vulnerability that the press didn't.
— A C (United Kingdom

The Garden Black

Prem creates verse that illuminates our world, its experiences and history.
—S C (United Kingdom)

Prem's poetry reminds that life is fragile and fleeting ... both harsh and beautiful.
—D G K (Canada)

A Few Places Near Home

The author has captured many beautiful images in this book, and is a wonderful photographer as well as a poet. This book would make a beautiful coffee table book filled with moving prose to make us ponder with gorgeous accompanying images.
—D K (Canada)

Author Information

Frank Prem has been a storytelling poet since his teenage years. He has been a psychiatric nurse through all of his professional career, which now exceeds forty years.

He has been published in magazines, online zines, and anthologies in Australia, and in a number of other countries, and has both performed and recorded his work as spoken word.

Frank is an Adjunct Research Associate of the School of Education, Charles Sturt University, Australia.

He lives with his wife in the beautiful township of Beechworth in North East Victoria, Australia.

Connect with Frank

Find Frank at his website www.FrankPrem.com, or through Social Media online at Facebook, X (Twitter), Instagram and YouTube.

Other Published Works

A Poetry Archive

A Poetry Archive – Volume 1 (2024)
A Poetry Archive – Volume 2 (2024)
A Poetry Archive – Volume 3 (2024)
A Poetry Archive – Volume 4 (2024)
A Poetry Archive – Volume 5 (2025)
A Poetry Archive – Volume 6 (2025)
A Poetry Archive – Volume 7 (2026)

Memoir

Small Town Kid (2018)
The New Asylum (2019)

Picture Poetry Series

Pilgrim Volume 1 - Illustrated by Leanne Murphy (2024)
A Lake Sambell Walk (2021)
A Few Places Near Home (2023)

Children's Picture Books

The Beechworth Bakery Bears (2021)
Waiting for Frank-Bear (2021)
On Allium Avenue (2025)

Bachelard Interpreted

A Choir of Whispers (2024).
A Cleansing Flame (2024)
Real Weight (2025)
A Flight Of Ideas (2025)
An Ocean of Purity (2025)
The Kiss Reverberant (2025)

Speculative Poetry

The Garden Black (2022)
A Specialist At The Recycled Heart (2022)
The Cielonaut (2024)

A Love Poetry Trilogy

Walk Away Silver Heart (2020)
A Kiss for the Worthy (2020)
Rescue and Redemption (2020)
Alive Is What You Feel (2023)

Natural Disasters

Devil In The Wind (2019)
Of Drought and Fire (2025)
SMALL Change (2025)

War and Conflict

Sheep On The Somme (2021)
From Volyn To Kherson (2023)

Free Verse

Pebbles to Poems (2020)
White Whale (2024)
Ida: Searching for The Jazz Baby (2023)
Herja, Devastation With Cage Dunn (2019)

Index of Poems

A

accordion (enough) 175
a good man (look at the camera) 257
a hot bath (feed the heater) 255
a house (yes it is) 213
ah well (the trough's under cover) 181
a little less cold (a little more mould) 55
alive and dead (outside their doors) 133
all I need (and my kookaburra) 23
all I needed (a lucky man) 27
almost educated (not likely) 71
almost enough rot-gut (and close-by to boot) 147
alone we die (in marion street) 157
a lullaby (of no harm tonight) 239
a meal costs a penny (if your dad doesn't work) 61
a memory (to take home) 31
a nine foot wingspan (would never fit) 59
an old bag (but it helps) 89
a place for the kiddies (to play) 151
a place (in the fitzroy night) 155
a place to play (if you know what I mean) 153
a shank's pony ride (from little barkly street) 43
a straitened alley (a straitened supper) 231
a tombstone fence (with pickets) 15
a tumbledown alley (a mostly-dry home) 41
a whistle (through the hessian) 233

B

bad dreams (are dreamt in twilight) 207
bail the bath (and seal the door) 115
bloody eyesore (to live in) 235
but (we couldn't anyway) 241

C

chicken wire (to feel safer in the night) 141
company (at mealtimes) 271
cricket and dogs and kids (and hopscotch) 69

D

damp enough (to make you sick) 187

E

everything (and our children) 45

F

for something better (but they don't mind) 125
from where they live (they're all vermin) 245

G

getting by (at a shilling a foot) 57
getting by (in the dudley mansions) 19
god and the brotherhood and the rain (to watch over us) 149
good neighbours (and close) 9

H

hard for the weather (to find us) 53
hardwicke street (tenements up into the sky) 173
hell to hang (inside) 105
hessian and paper (none at all) 113
he very devil (that leaves you numbed) 145
higgle and piggle (in north melbourne) 209
high and mighty (in hood street) 107
ho ho ho (for little children) 249
home (in the cobblestones) 67

I

I live here (in collingwood) 81
in and out (like a ginger beer stopper) 95
it'll do (until something better) 159
it means nothing (when it has always been) 189
it's all right (if you can't see the damp) 167
it's no good (half asleep) 195
it takes all the air (to breathe) 121

J

just like that (bastard) 179
just shut up (and do) 97

L

life in a doll house (of some sort anyway) 267
little charles we hope for (and bread) 85
love your neighbour (keep no secrets) 261
lucky children (with horses) 47

M

measles that bite (in the night-time) 39
mind your own (and draw the awning down) 205
more damage (as if) 111
more or less (it is whole) 221
my bible and god (first) 269

N

no complaints (the walls are thin) 75
no harm (walk to school) 275
no I repeat no (slums in fitzroy) 129
no one (nothing) 65
no one (to say boo) 73
no point complaining (no one will listen) 135
no room so (that's fair) 201
not in a window (maybe in a bottle) 109
not on your shoes (or legs) 215
not proud (but our best) 123
not quite (like the parliament) 265
no trouble (do they) 273

O

ooh look (the premier has come) 87

P

packed in (a good proposition) 119
pretty (the sty) 237
proper buggery (in a storm) 33
push and push back (it was war in little napier) 143

Q

quiet sunshine (ten minutes a day) 185
quite cosy (really) 281

R

rats (that come a-calling) 177
right at the door (marvelous) 259

S

saddle up (it's the same again) 285
say it (carlton) 37
shabby (is the gift) 243
shelter wood (from all storms) 51
singing (like you're dying) 225
slippy to the lavatory (in the winter) 77
something chronic (the key's not out) 137
still like convicts (more or less) 223
storm (in a tea-cup) by the water 29
sunshine and fresh air (for the bedding) 91
surprisingly good (for a sieve) 279
sweet sounds (in the backyard) 49

T

ten to her the rest to me (and the metho) 161
that's all right (nobody looks) 63
the beating heart (a place of pride) 131
the best we can (or eaten alive) 117
the hole is an odour (I'll have to fix myself) 253
the rat goes on (forever) 193
there are some (with gutter) 203
there are worse (we survive) 183
there's no kitchens (if you're on the susso) 139
the smell runs down the centre (of loughnan street) 13
the sun shines somewhere (not here) 171
three by three no bathroom (in argyle street) 165
tin is cold (so we do what we must) 163
tin (not gingerbread) 199
to keep out (of the night) 83
to the copper (all the money went) 191

U

undeserving (but shop I must) 21
up and down (a little love goes) 229
up the street (with cricket) 11

useless in the wet (and a trial through summer) 101

V

very close (in glasgow street) 99

W

washing day (kids out clothes in) 217
waste not (on temporary measures) 263
we can be clean (at least) 251
we will survive (baby mine) 197
whatever and wherever (a tin house) 277
what it is (is hunger) 25
what we have to do (top-to-toe) 103
where else? (right there) 219
whichever way you look (it's a lot of mouths) 93
will you (come and listen) 5
worth something (a little) 247

www.FrankPrem.com

www.ingramcontent.com/pod-product-compliance
Lightning Source LLC
Chambersburg PA
CBHW040046100526
44584CB00034BA/4497